indian cooking

delicious easy-to-make indian recipes

Contents

Text by James Phillips

This edition published in 2010 by L&K Designs.

© L&K Designs 2010

PRINTED IN CHINA

Publishers Disclaimer

The recipes contained in this book are passed on in good faith but the publisher cannot be held responsible for any adverse results. Please be aware that certain recipes may contain nuts.

Indian Cooking

When we think of Indian, a lot of us may automatically think of getting a takeaway on a Friday night. But Indian cuisine is more than that - it's a huge variety of spices, smells, textures and tastes.

Made ever more popular around the world by the availability of all the necessary ingredients, it is now easier than ever to create your own Indian menu from the comfort of your own home.

Making an Indian meal is often thought of as a culinary challenge, but in fact it is now very much accessible to all households, with most supermarkets stocking the basic ingredients. The easy-to-follow recipes make for a relatively stress-free way of 'spicing' things up in the kitchen.

The Indian diet as a whole is a healthy one, with lots of fresh fruit and vegetables in many curries, plus fresh fish, seafood, and a healthy balance of meats.

Indian food's popularity continues to grow, and more and more people are cooking Indian dishes for themselves at home now. This book is packed with delicious easy to make recipes for busy cooks as well as for those seeking a new challenge.

Spices are, of course, one of the key ingredients for Indian recipes, and whilst you may not have heard of some of the spices used in Indian cooking, most are easily bought.

Divided into easy to use chapters, follow the recipes to make everything from a tasty snack to a delicious feast with main dishes, rice, breads, chutneys, raitas and many more.

Starters & Snacks

Batata Vada (Serves 2)

Potato Ball Ingredients
250g/9oz mashed potato (cooled)
salt and freshly ground black pepper
1/4 tsp crushed dried chilli
1/2 tsp roasted coriander seeds
1 tsp chopped fresh ginger
1/2 tsp roasted cumin seeds

Batter Ingredients
180g/6 1/2oz gram flour (also known as chickpea/besan flour)
70g/2 1/2oz rice flour
1 1/2 tsps garlic and ginger paste (made by blending 1 garlic clove and
1cm/1/2-inch piece ginger with 1 tsp water to a paste in a food processor)
1/2 tsp crushed dried chilli
1 fenugreek leaf (chopped)
salt and freshly ground black pepper
water, as necessary

Directions
1. For the potato balls, mix all of the potato ball ingredients together in a
large bowl until well combined. Using your hands, roll the mixture into balls
about 4cm/1 1/2-inches in diameter. Set aside.

2. For the batter, in a separate bowl, mix together all of the batter
ingredients apart from the water and the vegetable oil. Gradually add
water as necessary, whisking the mixture continuously, until a batter with the
consistency of lightly whipped double cream forms.

3. Heat the oil in a deep heavy-based frying pan. Dip each of the potato
balls into the batter, then lower the balls into the hot oil in batches. Deep fry
for 3-4 minutes, or until the batter is crisp and golden-brown.

4. Remove the balls from the oil using a slotted spoon and set aside to drain
on kitchen paper. Repeat the process with the remaining potato balls.
To serve, place on a large serving plate. Serve mint chutney or tamarind
chutney in dipping bowls alongside. See raitas and chutney section for
recipes.

Onion Bhaji

Ingredients

1 onion, peeled
1/4 tsp coriander seeds
1/4 tsp cumin seeds
1/4 tsp chilli flakes
50g/2oz plain flour
1 tbsp baking powder
vegetable oil, for deep frying

Directions

1. Heat a deep-fat fryer to 190C/375F/Gas Mark 5 or fill a large pan one-third full with vegetable oil. To test if oil is at the correct temperature, drop a small cube of bread in the oil. If it sizzles and turns golden the oil is ready to use.

2. Chop half the onion and slice the remaining half. Squeeze the onion to release the juice, then add in the remaining ingredients (except the oil) and bind together. If necessary add cold water a little at a time. Divide the mixture into four large balls, and deep-fry until crisp and golden.

Kashmiri Spicy Potatoes (Serves 4)

Ingredients

3-4 medium potatoes, preferably a red variety, washed
1-2 tbsps butter
salt and freshly ground black pepper
1/4 tsp red chilli powder

Directions

1. Prick the potatoes several times with a fork. Microwave on a high heat for approx 12-15 minutes, or until tender. Cut the cooked potatoes in half.

2. Heat the butter in a frying pan over a medium heat until it is foaming. Season the butter, then add the red chilli powder and stir well.

3. Add the potato, ensuring they are coated by the spiced butter. Fry for 2-3 minutes, then serve immediately.

Sweet & Sour Red Lentils (Serves 2)

Ingredients

250g/1 1/4 cups red lentils
1/4 tsp ground turmeric
2 tbsps mustard or any other vegetable oil
1/2 tsp brown mustard seeds
1/2 tsp panch phoran *
4 hot dried red chillies
1 bay leaf
1 1/2 tsps salt
2 tbsps thick tamarind paste or to taste
1 tbsp sugar or to taste

Directions

1. Wash the lentils in several changes of water until the water runs clear. Put them in a medium-sized pan with the turmeric and mix. Cover with 4 1/2 cups of water.

2. Bring the lentils to the boil over a medium-high heat. Reduce the heat to low, cover and simmer for 40 minutes or until the lentils are tender. Stir now and then during the last 10 minutes. When the lentils are cooked, mash with a spoon to a pulp-like consistency.

Sweet & Sour Red Lentils/cont.

3. Heat the oil in a large non-stick pan or wok over a medium-high heat. When hot, add the mustard seeds. As soon as they pop, a matter of seconds, add the panch phoran, chillies and a bay leaf. Stir and fry for 20 seconds or until the chillies darken in colour.

4. Add the cooked lentils, 150ml/5fl oz of water and the salt. Stir to mix. Add the tamarind paste, a little at a time to get the sourness you desire. Add just enough sugar to balance the sourness. Bring to the boil.

5. Turn the heat to low and simmer for 8-10 minutes. The finished dal should have the consisitency of a thick purée.

* Panch Phoron (Bengali Five-Spice)

The distinct aroma of Bengali cuisine is mostly due to the blend of spices known as panch phoron. Panch means "five" and phoron is "flavour" or "spice", hence the common translation "Bengali Five-Spice". Panch phoron is a colourful blend of flavourful seeds: the green of fennel seed, black mustard and nigella seeds, golden fenugreek and buff-coloured cumin seeds. Some variations may substitute anise for the fennel seeds or wild mustard for cumin, radhuni seed for mustard, and possibly black cumin for nigella.

Panch Phoron

Ingredients
1 tbsp nigella seeds
1 tbsp black mustard seeds
1 tbsp fenugreek seeds
1 tbsp fennel seeds
1 tbsp cumin seeds

Directions

1. Combine all spices in a jar, store away from heat and light. Panch phoron is also known by the following names; panch phora, panch puran, panchpuran, punch poran, punch puram, punchpuram

Goan Spiced Aubergines (Makes 6)

Ingredients

6 tbsps gram flour (also known as chickpea/besan flour)
3 tsps rice flour
1/2 tsp red chilli powder
2 tsps ground cumin
2 tsps ground coriander
1 tsp dried mango powder
salt, to taste
180ml/6fl oz cold water
2 medium aubergines (washed and cut into 0.5cm/1/4 inch rounds)
vegetable oil, for frying
15 fresh curry leaves, to garnish (optional)

Directions

1. Place the gram flour, rice flour, chilli powder, ground cumin, ground coriander and mango powder into a bowl. Season, to taste, with salt.

2. Gradually add the cold water, whisking continuously to form a batter with the consistency of single cream.

3. Heat the oil in a deep heavy-based frying pan until a breadcrumb sizzles and turns brown when dropped into it.

4. Dip the aubergine rounds into the batter one by one and carefully lower them into the hot oil in batches. Fry for 2-3 minutes on each side, or until crisp and golden-brown and completely cooked through. Remove from the oil with a slotted spoon and set aside to drain on kitchen paper. Keep warm on a hot plate. Repeat the process with the remaining aubergines.

5. Heat 1 tbsp of the oil in a separate frying pan over a medium heat. When the oil is hot, add the curry leaves and fry for 1-2 minutes, or until crisp. Remove from the pan with a slotted spoon and set aside to drain on kitchen paper, then sprinkle with a pinch of salt.

6. To serve, divide the spiced aubergines among six serving plates and garnish with the curry leaves.

Vegetable Pakoras (Serves 4)

Ingredients
50g/2oz self-raising flour
250g/1/2 lb gram flour (also known as chickpea/besan flour)
1/2 tsp red chilli powder
1 tsp garam masala
1 tsp tandoori masala powder (optional)
1 tbsp lemon juice
300g/10 1/2oz potatoes (peeled and cut into small pieces)
300g/10 1/2oz onions (finely chopped)
6-8 spinach leaves (finely chopped)
3 spring onions (trimmed & finely chopped)
handful fresh coriander leaves
1 tsp chopped green chilli
1 tsp salt
sunflower oil, for deep frying

Directions
1. Sift the gram flour and the self-raising flour into a bowl. Add the chilli powder, garam masala and tandoori masala powder, if using, and stir well to combine.

2. Add the lemon juice, then gradually add enough water to form a smooth batter. Set aside for 10-15 minutes.

3. Add all of the remaining ingredients except the sunflower oil to the batter mixture and mix well to coat the potatoes and onions.

4. Heat the oil in a deep heavy-based frying pan until a breadcrumb sizzles and turns brown when dropped into it.

5. When the oil is hot, carefully lower tablespoons of the batter mixture in batches into the oil and fry for 5-6 minutes, or until the pakoras are crisp and golden-brown and the vegetables have cooked through.

Serve immediately.

Indian Tomato Soup (Serves 4)

Ingredients
650g/1lb 7oz ripe tomatoes (chopped)
1 tbsp butter
1 tsp vegetable oil
1 large bay leaf
1 small onion (chopped)
1 celery stalk (chopped)
1 large carrot (chopped)
2 garlic cloves (finely chopped)
2cm piece ginger (peeled and cut into thin strips)
1 tbsp cornflour (mixed to a paste with a splash of water)
1 tsp sugar
1 tsp freshly ground black pepper
100ml/3 1/2 fl oz milk
300-400ml/10-12 fl oz water
salt, to taste

Directions
1. Heat the butter and the oil in a large non-stick pan over a medium heat. Add the bay leaf and fry for 20-30 seconds. Add the chopped onion, celery, carrot, garlic and ginger and stir well.

2. Cover the pan with a lid and fry for 10-12 minutes, stirring occasionally, until the vegetables have softened and the onions are pale golden-brown.

3. Add the cornflour paste and stir for 1-2 minutes (do not allow the cornflour to burn).

4. Add the chopped tomatoes, sugar, salt and black pepper. Bring the mixture to a boil then simmer for 20-30 minutes, or until the tomatoes have reduced to a thick pulp.

5. Turn up the heat and continue to cook the tomato mixture for 5-6 minutes, or until the tomato skins have turned golden-brown. Discard the bay leaf.

Indian Tomato Soup/cont.

6. Transfer the tomato mixture to a food processor and blend to a purée. Add the milk and water in a thin stream until the mixture has the consistency of double cream and is smooth and well combined (you may not need all of the water).

7. Return the soup to the pan and return to the boil. Serve with bread.

Indian Chickpea & Vegetable Soup (Serves 2)

Ingredients
1 tbsp vegetable oil
1 large onion (chopped)
1 tsp finely grated fresh root ginger
1 garlic clove (chopped)
1 tbsp garam masala
850ml/3 3/4 cups vegetable stock
2 large carrots (quartered lengthways and chopped)
400g/15oz can chickpeas (drained)
100g/4oz green beans (chopped)

Directions
1. Heat the oil in a medium saucepan, then add the onion, ginger and garlic. Fry for 2 minutes, then add the garam masala. After 1 minute, stir and then add the stock and carrots. Simmer for 10 minutes.

2. Add the chickpeas. Use a blender to whisk the soup a little. Stir in the beans and simmer for 3 minutes. Serve with naan bread.

Tandoori Chicken

Chicken Ingredients
1.25kg/2 1/2 lbs chicken pieces (legs and/or breasts) skinned
1 tsp salt
3 tbsps lemon juice

Marinade Ingredients
450ml/3/4 pint plain yoghurt
1/2 onion (coarsely chopped)
1 garlic clove (chopped)

2.5cm/1-inch piece fresh root ginger (chopped)
1-2 hot green chillies (roughly sliced)
2 tsps garam masala
lemon wedges, to serve

Directions
1. Cut each chicken leg into two pieces and each breast into four pieces. Make deep slits crossways on the meaty parts of each leg and breast piece.

2. Spread the chicken pieces out on two large platters. Sprinkle one side with half the salt and half the lemon juice and rub them in. Turn the pieces over and repeat on the second side. Set aside for 20 minutes.

3. Meanwhile, make the marinade: combine the yoghurt, onion, garlic, ginger, chillies and garam masala in a blender or food processor and blend until smooth. Strain the paste through a sieve into a large bowl, pushing through as much liquid as you can.

4. Put the chicken and all the juices into the bowl with the marinade. Rub the marinade into the slits in the meat, then cover and refrigerate for 24 hours.

5. Preheat the oven to its maximum temperature. Remove the chicken pieces from the marinade and spread them out in a single layer on a large, shallow, baking tray.

6. Bake for 20-25 minutes, until cooked through. Lift the chicken pieces out of their juices and serve with lemon wedges.

Kashmiri Lamb Kebabs (Makes 20)
Ingredients
500g/1lb 2oz lamb mince (minced extra fine)
1 free-range egg
1 thick slice white bread (crusts removed, blended to breadcrumbs in a food processor)
1/2 tsp ground turmeric
1/2 tsp red chilli powder

Kashmiri Lamb Kebabs/cont.

1 tsp ground cumin
1 tsp ginger paste (made by blending 1cm/1/2-inch piece of ginger in 1 tsp of water)
salt, to taste
2 tbsps Greek-style yoghurt
4 black cardamom pods (seeds only)
16 green cardamom pods (seeds only)
8 cloves
1cm/1/2-inch piece cinnamon
4 tbsps vegetable oil

Directions

1. Place all of the ingredients except the oil into a mixing bowl and mix together until well combined.

2. Divide the mixture into small portions and, using your hands, roll each portion into a ball, then flatten into a patty.

3. Heat one and a half tablespoons of the oil in a frying pan over a medium heat. Add half of the kebab patties and fry for 3-4 minutes on each side, or until golden-brown on all sides and cooked though the middle.

4. Remove the kebab patties from the oil using a slotted spoon and set aside to drain on kitchen paper.

5. Repeat the process with the remaining kebab patties, and place onto skewers to serve, with pre-prepared vegetables if desired.

Paneer Stuffed Peppers (Serves 4-6)

Ingredients

4 large red or green peppers (stalks removed, flesh cut in half, seeds scooped out)
4 tbsps vegetable oil
1 1/2 tsps cumin seeds
1 onion (chopped)
3 large tomatoes (chopped)
2 tsps finely chopped ginger
2 handfuls frozen peas
70g/2 1/2oz green beans (chopped)
1/2 tsp ground turmeric
1/2 tsp red chilli powder
2 tsps ground coriander
1 1/2 tsps garam masala
250g/9oz fresh paneer (crumbled) *
100ml/3 1/2 fl oz water
5 tbsps double cream
handful fresh chopped coriander
200g/7oz basmati rice (cooked according to packet instructions) to serve
salt, to taste

Directions

1. Preheat the oven to 190C/375F/Gas Mark 5. Place the pepper halves onto a baking tray, drizzle with one tablespoon of the oil and bake in the oven for 20-25 minutes, or until softened. Once the peppers are cooked, remove them from the oven and set aside.

2. Meanwhile, heat the remaining oil in a non-stick pan. Add the cumin seeds and fry for 20-30 seconds, or until fragrant. Add the chopped onion and cook for 3-4 minutes, or until golden-brown.

Paneer Stuffed Peppers/cont.

3. Add the tomatoes, ginger, peas, beans, salt and spices and simmer for 10-12 minutes, or until the tomatoes have softened and reduced to a pulp.

4. Add the crumbled paneer and the water and stir until well combined. Bring the mixture to a simmer and simmer for 2-3 minutes. Add the double cream and season well with freshly ground black pepper. Simmer until heated through.

5. Add the chopped coriander and continue to simmer the mixture for 4-5 minutes, adding tablespoons of water as necessary to stop the sauce from drying out as the paneer absorbs the liquid.

6. Preheat the grill to its highest setting. While the grill is heating up, fill each of the baked pepper halves with the paneer mixture. When the grill is hot, grill the stuffed peppers until the paneer mixture is golden-brown. To serve, place one or two stuffed pepper halves onto each serving plate. Spoon a portion of basmati rice alongside each.

* Paneer is an indian cheese.

Gujarati Potatoes with Cashew Nuts (Makes 3-4)

Ingredients
300ml/1/2 pint vegetable oil (for deep frying, plus 1 tbsp, for frying)
450g/1lb potatoes (peeled and cut into fries)
1/2 tsp ground turmeric
1/2 tsp red chilli powder
1 tsp sugar
3/4 tsp dried mango powder
1 tsp ground cumin
2 tbsps cashew nuts
1 tbsp sesame seeds
salt, to taste

Directions
1. Heat the oil in a deep heavy-based frying pan until a breadcrumb sizzles and turns brown when dropped into it.

2. When the oil is hot enough, add the potatoes and fry over a medium heat for 5-7 minutes, or until just tender. Add the turmeric, red chilli powder, salt, sugar, dried mango powder and cumin to the pan.

3. Turn up the flame and continue to fry for 3-4 minutes, or until the potatoes are crisp and golden-brown. Remove the potatoes from the pan using a slotted spoon and set aside to drain on kitchen paper.

4. Meanwhile, in a separate frying pan, heat 1 tbsp of the oil over a medium heat, add the cashew nuts and fry for 1-2 minutes, or until golden-brown.

5. Add the sesame seeds and fry for a further minute, or until the sesame seeds are golden-brown.

6. To serve, place the potatoes into a serving dish. Pour over the fried nuts and seeds and stir well to coat the potatoes in them.

Serve immediately.

Vegetable Samosas (Makes 24)

Ingredients - Pastry
750g/6 1/2 cups of plain flour
375ml/1 2/3 cups of warm water
6 tbsps butter (melted)
salt (to season)

Ingredients - Filling
8 medium-sized potatoes (boiled in skins and cooled)
2 fresh green chilli peppers (chopped)
1 tsp chilli powder
2 tbsps vegetable oil
2 tsps cumin seeds
1 1/2 tsps chat masala spice
1 1/2 lemons, juiced
handful of fresh coriander (chopped)
salt (to season)

Vegetable Samosas/cont.

Directions - Pastry

1. Sift the salt and plain flour into a bowl and add the melted butter. Add some warm water to the mixture, enough to make a firm dough. Mix together, kneading the dough gently until smoothed out. Turn the dough out and wrap with cling wrap. Set aside for 30 minutes.

Directions - Filling

1. Peel the already cooked and cooled potatoes and place them in a large pan. Mash them coarsely. Heat the oil in a large saucepan and add the cumin seeds, cook them for 1 minute, until fragrant. Stir in the chilli powder, ginger, mashed potato and chilli pepper; cook for 2-3 minutes, stirring frequently.

2. Add the chat masala, salt, lemon juice and fresh coriander, mixing them in well. Remove the saucepan from the heat and leave to cool. Lightly flour a clean work surface and take the dough out of the cling wrap and divide into 12 equally sized pieces. Roll each piece into an oval shape, about 9 inches by 5 inches. Cut each piece in half, crossways.

3. Take one of the halves in your palm, with the straight cut-edge along your forefinger. Wet your other hand and run it along the straight edge. Place the 4 fingers of your free hand in the centre of the oval half and fold in the sides, (using the fingers underneath the pastry) – creating a cone-shape. Press the overlapping edges down to seal the pastry.

4. Hold the cone with the open end at the top, cone point at the bottom and spoon some of the cooled filling mixture inside, to about 2/3 full. Pinch the edges of the opening together, to seal the pastry completely.

5. Place onto a floured baking tray, to avoid sticking. Repeat this process with the remaining dough and filling.

6. Pour about 5 inches of vegetable oil into a wok or karahi and heat to about 190C/375F/Gas Mark 5. Place 4-5 samosas in the heated oil at a time and cook for 4-5 minutes, turning them frequently. Remove with a slotted spoon and drain on kitchen paper towel. Serve immediately.

Fish & Seafood

Super-Quick Fish Curry (Serves 6)

Ingredients

675g/1 1/2 lb cod fillet, or other white fish (cut into 1 inch chunks)
620g/2 3/4 cups of canned, chopped tomatoes
3 tbsps Balti or Madras curry paste
1 large onion (finely sliced)
2 tbsps vegetable oil
Handful of coriander leaves (chopped)

Directions

1. Heat the vegetable oil in a large frying pan and add the onion. Cook for 3-4 minutes, until tender. Add the curry paste and cook for a further 2 minutes.

2. Add the chopped tomatoes and bring just to the boil. Reduce the heat and simmer for 10-15 minutes, until the sauce has thickened.

3. Add the fish chunks and continue to simmer for 3-5 minutes, until the fish is cooked.

4. Remove from the heat and sprinkle coriander leaves over the top. Serve immediately with hot rice.

One-Pot Cod and Prawn Curry (Serves 6)

Ingredients

675g/1 1/2 lb cod fillet, or other white fish (cut into 1 inch chunks)
250g/9oz prawns (cooked and peeled)
225ml/1 cup of canned coconut milk
7 tbsps green masala curry paste
2-3 sprigs of fresh coriander (to garnish)

Directions

1. Place the curry paste and coconut milk in a large saucepan and bring just to the boil. Reduce the heat and simmer for 4-5 minutes, stirring occasionally.

2. Add the cod chunks and cook over a gentle heat for 4-5 minutes. Stir in the prawns and cook for 2-3 minutes, until heated through.

One-Pot Cod and Prawn Curry/cont.

3. Remove from the heat and serve immediately, topped with coriander sprigs.

Slow-Cook Salmon Curry (Serves 4-6)

Ingredients

500g/1 lb 2oz salmon fillet (skinless, deboned and cut into 1 inch chunks)
450ml/2 cups of hot vegetable stock (or chicken)
1 tbsp fish sauce
2 cloves of garlic (crushed)
3 shallots (finely chopped)
3/4 tsp dried chilli flakes
1 lemongrass stalk (finely chopped)
1 inch pieces of fresh root ginger (finely chopped)
1 tsp light muscovado sugar

Directions

1. To be cooked in a slow cooker. Place the salmon chunks in a bowl, cover and leave to stand at room temperature.

2. Turn the slow cooker to a high temperature and add the hot stock. Add the ginger, lemongrass, sugar, fish sauce, garlic, shallots and chilli flakes and combine well.

3. Cover the slow cooker and cook for 2-2 1/4 hours. Add a little more stock, if required.

4. Add the salmon chunks to the slow cooker re-cover and cook for 12-15 minutes. Turn the slow cooker off and leave the curry in the pot for a further 15 minutes, until the salmon is cooked through.

5. Serve immediately in serving bowls.

White Fish Curry (Serves 4)

Ingredients

500g/1 lb 2oz cooked cod fillets (cut into chunks)
1 tsp ground cumin
1 tsp chilli powder
1 tsp ground coriander
1 tsp ground turmeric
1 tsp ginger paste
1 bay leaf
1 onion (chopped)
2 fresh green chillies (chopped)
2 cloves of garlic (crushed)
125ml/1/2 cup of natural yoghurt
150ml/2/3 cup of water
3-4 tbsps vegetable oil
salt (to season)

Directions

1. Heat the oil in a large frying pan and add the onion. Cook for 3-4 minutes, until tender. Add the garlic, bay leaf and ginger and cook for 1 minute.

2. Stir in the spices and continue to cook for another minute. Pour in the yoghurt, followed by the chilli and water. Bring to the boil, reduce the heat and simmer for 3 minutes.

3. Add the cod pieces and season with salt. Cover the pan and simmer for 15 minutes. Remove the bay leaf before serving. Serve with hot, cooked rice.

Creamy Cod Curry (Serves 4-6)

Ingredients

500g/1 lb 2oz cod fillets (skinless, boneless and cut into chunks)
250ml/1 cup of natural yoghurt
60ml/1/4 cup of double cream
2 onions (chopped)
2 cloves of garlic (crushed)
1 tsp turmeric

Creamy Cod Curry/cont.

2 tsps garam masala

3 tsps ground coriander

2 tsps gram flour (also known as chickpea/besan flour)

3 tbsps vegetable oil

1 inch piece of fresh root ginger (grated)

2 tbsps boiling water

pinch of saffron threads

1/4 tsp salt

1/4 tsp cayenne pepper

Directions

1. Place the saffron threads in a small bowl and cover with water; leave to soak for 5 minutes.

2. Heat the vegetable oil in a large saucepan and add the onions. Cook for 4-5 minutes, until tender.

3. Add the turmeric, coriander, garam masala, garlic, ginger, cayenne pepper and salt; cook for 1 minute, stirring frequently. Add the flour and stir in well, cooking for 1 more minute. Remove from the heat.

4. Pour the double cream and yoghurt into the saucepan and return to heat. Gradually bring to the boil and add the saffron, (with the soaking water), and the fish chunks.

5. Reduce the heat, cover and simmer for 12-15 minutes, until the fish is cooked and flakes easily with a fork.

6. Serve immediately with boiled rice.

Red Prawn Curry (Serves 4-6)

Ingredients - Curry Paste

2 tbsps red curry paste

2 cloves of garlic (crushed)

1 inch piece of fresh root ginger (finely chopped)

2 onions (chopped)

1 tbsp fresh coriander leaves (chopped)

Ingredients - Curry

500g/1 lb 2oz cooked and peeled prawns
500g/1 lb 2oz mixed vegetables
225ml/1 cup of thick coconut milk
3 tbsps vegetable oil
1 tbsp sugar
salt (to season)

Directions

1. Place the red curry paste, garlic, ginger, onions and coriander leaves in a food processor and blend into a paste.

2. Heat the vegetable oil in a large saucepan and stir in the paste. Cook for 3-5 minutes. Pour in the coconut milk and sugar and bring to the boil.

3. Stir in the vegetables and prawns and simmer for 3-5 minutes. Season with a little salt, according to taste. Remove from the heat and serve immediately with hot rice.

Mixed Seafood Curry (Serves 6)

Ingredients

750g/1lb 4oz halibut (cut into chunks)
300g/11oz squid (cleaned, tentacles removed)
18 fresh clams (in shells, cleaned)
300g/11oz tiger prawns (raw, peeled and deveined)
6 shallots (finely chopped)
3 tbsps curry paste
1 1/2 tbsps vegetable oil
2 cloves of garlic (crushed)
1 1/2 tsps shrimp paste
750ml/3 1/3 cups of coconut milk
8 fresh basil leaves (finely shredded)

Directions

1. Cut the squid body 'shells' into thick rings.

2. Heat the vegetable oil in a preheated wok and add the garlic, shallots and curry paste. Stir-fry for 2-3 minutes.

Mixed Seafood Curry/cont.

3. Stir in the shrimp paste and add the coconut milk; bring to the boil. Reduce the heat to a simmer and add the prawns, squid and halibut and simmer for 2-3 minutes.

4. Add the clams in their shells and simmer for 1-2 minutes, until the clams open. Remove any clam shells which fail to open.

5. Remove from the heat and stir in the basil leaves. Serve with hot rice.

Sweet and Spicy Monkfish Curry (Serves 6)

Ingredients

750g/1lb 4oz monkfish (cut into 1 inch cubes)
450ml/2 cups of coconut milk
1 medium pineapple (peeled and cut into 1 inch cubes)
3 dried chillies (chopped)
4 cloves of garlic (finely sliced)
5cm piece of fresh ginger (finely sliced)
1 lime, juiced
65-75ml/1/3 cup of cold water
3 red peppers (sliced)
3 tsps chilli powder
1 tsp turmeric
1 tsp ground cumin
1/2 tsp salt
3 tbsps vegetable oil

Directions

1. Place the dried chillies, turmeric, salt, cumin and chilli powder in a bowl and mix into a paste. Set to one side.

2. Heat the vegetable oil in a large frying pan and add the garlic, ginger and sliced red peppers. Stir-fry on a medium/high heat for 4-5 minutes.

3. Stir in the pineapple and cook for 1 minute. Stir in the spice paste and continue to stir-fry for 1-2 minutes.

4. Add the monkfish chunks and the coconut milk and bring the mixture to just boiling. Reduce the heat and simmer for 5-7 minutes, until the monkfish is cooked.

5. When cooked, stir in the lime juice and remove from the heat. Serve immediately.

Spiced Whitebait (Serves 4)

Ingredients
400g/14oz whitebait
1-2 tbsps rock salt
1 lime, juiced
1 tsp ground turmeric
2 tsps red chilli powder
1 tsp ground cumin
1cm/1/2-inch piece fresh root ginger (peeled and chopped)
3 garlic cloves (chopped)
50g/1 3/4 oz plain flour
50g/1 3/4 oz gram flour (also known as chickpea/besan flour)
2 tsps rice flour
fine salt, to taste
4 tbsps vegetable oil

Directions
1. Rub the whitebait with the rock salt to remove the scales. Wash and drain the fish, then rub it all over with the lime juice and ground spices. Grind the root ginger and chopped garlic to a paste using a mortar and pestle.

2. In a bowl, mix the plain flour, gram flour, rice flour and ginger and garlic paste together until well combined. Season, to taste, with fine salt. Dredge the whitebait in the flour mixture until it is completely coated.

3. Heat the oil in a frying pan or heavy wok over a medium heat, until smoking. Add the fish in batches and fry for 4-5 minutes on each side, or until crisp and golden-brown on all sides. Set each batch aside to drain on kitchen paper.

Serve immediately.

Prawn & Coconut Pilaf (Serves 4)

Ingredients

250g/9oz basmati rice
300g/10 1/2oz raw prawns (peeled)
2 large garlic cloves
2 medium tomatoes (quartered)
1 medium onion (finely sliced)
1 small piece fresh root ginger (roughly chopped)
4 tbsps vegetable oil
1 tsp cumin seeds
5 black peppercorns
1/2 cinnamon stick
3 cloves
3 cardamom pods
1/2 tsp turmeric
1/2 tsp chilli powder
1 tsp ground coriander
handful of coconut flakes (to serve)

Directions

1. Cook the rice according to packet instructions, then set aside. Put the ginger, garlic and tomatoes into a food processor, blend to make a paste, then set aside until you're ready to cook.

2. Heat the oil in a large non-stick pan and add the whole spices. Once they start to sizzle, add the onion, frying over a medium heat for about 10 minutes until soft.

3. Add the ground spices and paste, then cook over a low heat, stirring until the sauce has released the oil back into the pan.

4. Add the prawns, then cook for a few minutes until cooked through - the mixture should be quite dry.

5. Stir the cooked rice into the pan to coat it well in the spices. Make sure the rice is heated through.

Serve scattered with the coconut flakes.

King Prawn & Almond Curry (Serves 4)

Ingredients
12 raw king prawns (peeled and de-veined, heads removed, tails on)
1 tbsp vegetable oil

Sauce Ingredients
100g/4oz cashews
50g/2oz blanched almonds
2 tbsps ghee or butter
1 bay leaf
2 green cardamom pods (crushed)
1 onion (finely chopped)
small knob of fresh ginger (peeled and finely chopped)
1 green chilli (chopped)
1/2 tsp turmeric
300ml/1/2 pint fish stock
small pinch of saffron strands, infused in 2 tbsps warm milk
1 tsp golden caster sugar
2 tbsps single cream
pinch of garam masala

First Marinade Ingredients
small knob of fresh ginger (peeled and finely grated or blended to a paste)
2 garlic cloves (very finely grated or blended to a paste)
1/2 tsp ground white pepper
1/2 tsp turmeric

Second Marinade Ingredients
2 tbsps single cream
2 tbsps Greek yoghurt
pinch of saffron strands (soaked in 2 tbsps warm milk for 5 minutes)
4 green cardamom pods and 2 pieces of mace (ground together)
1/2 tsp cumin seeds

Directions
1. To make the sauce, tip the cashews and almonds into a saucepan and just cover with cold water. Boil gently for 20 minutes until slightly softened. Tip the nuts and water into a food processor and blend.

King Prawns & Almond Curry/cont.

2. Heat the ghee or butter in a heavy saucepan, add the bay leaf, cardamoms and onion and fry for 8-10 minutes until golden. Add the ginger and chilli and fry for a minute until fragrant.

3. Add the turmeric and fry until the onion turns yellow, which should take another minute. Now stir in the nut purée and cook the paste carefully, stirring regularly until yellow. Pour in 150ml of the fish stock and simmer for 2-3 minutes.

4. As the sauce turns glossy, add the infused saffron, sugar and cream, sprinkle in the garam masala and season with salt. Simmer for a few more minutes. The sauce should be too thick to pour, but thin enough to spoon, so you may need to dilute it with more fish stock. (The sauce can be made up to an hour ahead.)

5. Tip the prawns into a bowl, and mix in a sprinkling of salt and all the ingredients for the first marinade. If this looks dry, add a drop of water. Set aside for 10 minutes.

6. Heat the oil in a large pan and sear the prawns for 20 seconds so they curl up. Remove and set aside to cool.

7. Mix the ingredients together for the second marinade, then toss the prawns in it (they can be left for up to 1 hour).

8. Preheat the oven to fan 180C/350F/Gas Mark 4. Pierce a long wooden skewer through the tail of each prawn and thread it through to the tip of the head.

9. Meanwhile, reheat the sauce and add more stock if it is too thick.

10. Serve the prawns on a large plate in a pool of sauce for people to help themselves, with the extra sauce and pilau rice in bowls.

Meat Curries

Beef Vindaloo (Serves 4)

Ingredients

975g/6 1/2 cups of beef (diced)
2 onions (finely sliced)
4 cloves of garlic (finely chopped)
3 large, ripe tomatoes (chopped)
5-10 dried red chillies (depending on taste)
3 large green chillies (chopped)
1 tsp brown sugar
6cm piece of fresh cinnamon
3cm piece of fresh ginger (grated)
1 tsp ground cumin
1/2 tsp ground turmeric
1 tsp coriander seeds
1 tsp black pepper
1 tsp salt
1/4 tsp cloves
1/4 tsp cardamom seeds
1/4 tsp fenugreek seeds (soaked in boiling water for 30 mins)
5-6 tbsps malt vinegar
2 tbsps vegetable oil
1 1/2 litres of water

Directions

1. Using a pestle and mortar (or an electric spice grinder) grind the cloves, cinnamon, coriander seeds, turmeric, salt, black pepper, cardamom, cumin fenugreek seeds and dried red chillies. Place them in a large bowl and mix together well.

2. Add the vinegar and beef to the bowl of spices and coat the beef well. Cover and refrigerate for 2-3 hours.

3. Heat the vegetable oil in a large saucepan and add the onions. Cook over a medium heat for 3-4 minutes, until slightly browned. Increase the heat a little and add the chillies, ginger, tomatoes and garlic. Cook for 2-3 minutes.

Beef Vindaloo/cont.

4. Add the coated beef cubes and cook for 2-3 minutes, until browned. Add the remaining marinade and cover with cold water, covering the beef by at least 1cm. Bring to the boil.

5. Reduce the heat, partially cover with a lid and simmer gently for 1 1/2 hours, stirring occasionally and checking the beef to ensure it becomes tender. If not tender after 1 1/2 hours, add 110ml of water and simmer for an additional 30-45 minutes.

6. Once ready, add the sugar, stirring it in well. Serve immediately with hot rice and cucumber and mint raita (see recipe on page 82).

Lamb Korma (Serves 6)

Ingredients
1kg boneless leg of lamb (trimmed and cut into 2 inch cubes)
375ml/1 2/3 cup of single cream
55g/1/4 cup of vegetable oil
9 tsps garam masala
1 1/2 large onions (finely chopped)
2-3 tbsps cashew nut masala
4-5 dried red chillies (deseeded and crushed)
1 1/2 inch fresh root ginger (grated)
3 tsps lemon juice
1 1/2 tbsps fresh coriander leaves (chopped)
salt (to season)

Directions
1. Heat the oil in a large saucepan and add the lamb cubes. Cook for 3-4 minutes, until browned. Add the onion and cook for 4-5 minutes, stirring frequently.

2. Add the ginger, chillies, garam masala and the cashew nut masala. Cook for 2-3 minutes.

3. Stir in the cream, chopped coriander and 110ml of water. Season with salt, according to taste. Bring to the boil.

4. Reduce the heat, cover and simmer for 50-60 minutes, until the lamb is tender. Add the lemon juice, stirring it in well. Remove from the heat and serve with hot rice.

Lamb Madras (Serves 6-8)

Ingredients
900g/2llb lamb shoulder (trimmed and cut into cubes)
2-3 onions (diced)
3 cloves of garlic (crushed)
225ml/1 cup of vegetable oil
1.8 litres/8 cups of lamb or chicken stock
2 tbsps garam masala
2 tsps dried red pepper flakes
2 tbsps black mustard seeds
2 tsps ground cumin
2 tsps turmeric
2 tsps ground cardamom
salt and black pepper
2-4 tbsps plain yoghurt

Directions
1. Place the lamb cubes in a bowl and season with salt and black pepper; tossing the cubes to ensure even coverage.

2. Heat the lamb oil in a large saucepan and add the seasoned lamb. Cook over a high heat for 3-5 minutes, until lightly browned on all sides. Remove the lamb with a slotted spoon and set aside.

Lamb Madras/cont.

3. Reduce the heat to a medium/high setting and add the garlic and onions. Cook for 3-4 minutes, until the onions are tender. Reduce the heat again, to a medium setting and stir in the dried spices. Cook for 2-3 minutes, stirring frequently.

4. Return the lamb to the saucepan, followed by the lamb stock. Bring to the boil, then reduce the heat and simmer for 1 1/4 - 1 1/2 hours. Regularly skim any fat that lays on the top of the mixture and discard.

Serve with basmati rice and choice of breads. Garnish with plain yoghurt, according to taste.

Lamb Rogan Josh (Serves 6-8)

Ingredients
900g/2lb lamb fillet (cut into cubes)
250ml/1 cup of natural yoghurt
2 onions (thinly sliced)
2 cloves of garlic (crushed)
1 inch piece of fresh root ginger (grated)
6 tomatoes (skinned and chopped)
1 red pepper (1/2 sliced finely and half sliced in long strips)
1 green pepper (1/2 sliced finely and half sliced in long strips)
3 green cardamoms (crushed)
2 tsps chilli powder
2 tsps paprika
2 tsps turmeric
2 tsps ground coriander
2 tsps ground cumin
75ml vegetable oil
1/2 tsp salt

Directions
1. Heat 50ml/1/4 cup of the oil in a large saucepan and add the garlic, onion and ginger. Cook for 4-5 minutes, until tender and lightly browned. Stir in the spices and fry gently for 2 minutes, stirring continuously.

2. Increase the heat a little and add the lamb cubes. Cook for 3-4 minutes, browning the meat on all sides.

3. Reserve 60ml/1/4 cup of the yoghurt and gradually add the remaining yoghurt to the saucepan, 1 tbsp at a time, stirring continuously and combining before adding the next tablespoon.

4. Stir the salt into the saucepan followed by the finely chopped red and green peppers and 4 of the chopped tomatoes. Cook for 3-4 minutes, over a medium or high heat, tossing all the ingredients together.

5. Reduce the heat, cover and simmer for 1-1 1/2 hours, until the meat is tender, stirring the mixture every 20 minutes, to prevent sticking.

6. Towards the end of cooking, heat the remaining oil in a frying pan and add the strips of green and red pepper. Cook for 3-4 minutes, until softening. Add the remaining chopped tomatoes and add a pinch of salt. Cook over a medium/high heat, tossing the ingredients together.

7. Transfer the cooked curry into a serving dish and top with the pepper/onion mixture.

Drizzle over the remaining yoghurt and serve immediately with hot rice.

Indian-Style Pork Curry (Serves 6-8)

Ingredients - Curry Paste
1 1/2 tbsps garam masala powder
10 red chillies (split and deseeded)
4 cloves of garlic (finely chopped)
4cm fresh ginger (finely chopped)
1 large onion (sliced)
110ml/1/2 cup of malt vinegar
4 tbsps vegetable oil

Ingredients - Curry
900g/2 lb boneless pork shoulder (cubed)
1 tsp turmeric
1 tsp salt
3-4 red chillies (whole)

Directions
1. Place the turmeric and salt in a large bowl and mix together. Add the pork cubes and coat with the mixture. Set to one side.

2. Place the deseeded chillies in a bowl and cover with very hot water. Leave to soak for 8-10 minutes. Pour the liquid and chillies into a food processor and blend, until coarsely chopped. Add the ginger, garam masala, vinegar, onion and garlic and blend until smooth.

3. Heat the vegetable oil in a large saucepan and add the seasoned pork. Cook for 2-3 minutes, until browned. Add the curry paste and stir together well, coating all the pork.

4. Add enough hot water to cover the pork and bring to the boil. Reduce the heat, cover and simmer for 35-45 minutes, until the pork is tender and the sauce has reduced enough.

5. Serve immediately over hot rice and top with the whole red chillies.

North-Indian Lamb Curry (Serves 4-6)

Ingredients

550g/1lb 3oz lamb (boneless and cubed)
1.5 litres/7 cups of water
60g/3 1/2oz yellow split peas
1 large onion (sliced)
2 fresh green chillies (chopped)
2 cloves of garlic (crushed)
3 black peppercorns
1 bay leaf
1 cinnamon stick
1/2 tsp ground turmeric
1 3/4 tsps chilli powder
1 tsp ground coriander seeds
2 cloves
1 tsp salt
1 tbsp fresh coriander (chopped)
4 tbsps vegetable oil

Directions

1. Heat the oil in a large saucepan and add the onion, peppercorns, cloves and bay leaf. Cook for 4-5 minutes, until the onion is tender and lightly browned.

2. Add the lamb and stir in the coriander seeds, cinnamon, garlic, turmeric and chilli. Stir together well and then season with 3/4 tsp salt. Stir-fry over a medium heat for 5-6 minutes. Pour 950ml/4 cups of the water into the saucepan and bring to the boil. Reduce the heat, cover and simmer for 40-45 minutes, until the lamb is cooked and tender.

3. Place the split peas in a large pan and cover with the remaining water. Add the remaining salt and bring to the boil. Boil for 13-15 minutes, until the water has reduced down and the peas are soft, (add more water, if required, throughout cooking).

4. Remove the lamb mixture from the heat stir the split peas in mixing them in well. Stir in the green chillies and coriander. Serve immediately.

Lamb Biryani (Serves 4)

Ingredients

500g/1lb 2oz lean lamb leg steak (cubed)
200g/7oz basmati rice (rinsed in cold water)
400ml/1 3/4 cups lamb stock
1 tbsp balti curry paste
200g/7oz spinach

Directions

1. Heat a large pan and fry the curry paste until fragrant, add the lamb, then brown on all sides.

2. Pour in the rice and stock, then stir well. Bring to the boil, cover with a lid, then cook for 15 minutes on a medium heat until the rice is tender.

3. Stir through the spinach, put the lid back on the pan and leave to steam, undisturbed, for 5 minutes before serving.

Lamb Saag (Serves 6)

Ingredients

750g/1 1/2 lbs lamb shoulder (fat trimmed off)
3 garlic cloves (peeled)
large piece of ginger (roughly chopped)
2-3 green chillies (roughly chopped)
2 cardamom pods (squashed)
4 large tomatoes (quartered)
1 large onion (roughly chopped)
2 tsps coriander seeds (toasted and ground)
1 tsp turmeric
300m/1 1/4 cups lamb stock
200g/7oz spinach (washed and roughly chopped)
2 tsps cumin seeds (toasted and ground)

Directions

1. Put the garlic, ginger, chillies and onion into a small food processor and whisk into a purée (or you could very finely chop everything, but blending is easier).

2. Heat a teaspoon of oil in a large casserole dish. Brown the lamb all over and scoop out. Fry the spices in the same pan for a couple of minutes until fragrant then add the onion purée and cook for 2 minutes. Add the lamb, tomatoes and stock. Stir, cover and cook for 45 minutes.

3. Stir in the spinach then cook for a further 40 minutes or until the lamb is tender. Scatter the coriander over.

Serve with naan breads or basmati rice.

Pork Vindaloo (Serves 3-4)

Ingredients
350g/12oz pork shoulder (flesh cut into 2.5cm/1-inch cubes)
100g/3 1/2oz pork belly (cut into 2.5cm/1-inch pieces)
1 tsp cumin seeds
1 tsp coriander seeds
65ml/1/4 cup vegetable oil
5 black peppercorns (whole)
2 green cardamom pods (seeds only)
7 garlic cloves (peeled and whole)
2 cloves
1cm/1/2-inch piece cinnamon
1cm/1/2-inch piece ginger (peeled and chopped)
3 fresh red chillies
3 tbsps white wine vinegar
1 tsp salt
1 small onion, finely chopped
3/4 tsp mustard seeds
handful of cashew nuts

Directions
1. Using a spice grinder, grind the cumin seeds, coriander seeds, peppercorns, cardamom seeds, cloves and cinnamon to a fine powder.

2. In a food processor, blend the ginger, garlic, chillies and white wine vinegar to a paste. Mix the spices with the paste until well combined and season with a pinch of salt. Rub the mixture all over the pork using your fingers, then set the pork aside, covered, to marinate for 2 hours.

Pork Vindaloo/cont.

3. Heat four tablespoons of the oil in a non-stick pan. When the oil is hot, add the onion and fry for 3-4 minutes, or until golden-brown.

4. Add the marinated pork pieces and fry for 6-7 minutes, turning once, until golden-brown on all sides.

5. Reduce the heat to low, cover the pan with a lid and cook for 35-40 minutes, stirring occasionally, or until the pork is tender. Add small splashes of boiling water to the pan as necessary if the juices in the pan dry out. Add as little water as possible as the resulting sauce should be quite thick.

6. Heat the remaining teaspoon of oil in a separate pan over a medium heat. When the oil is hot, add the mustard seeds.

7. Once the mustard seeds start to pop, add the cashew nuts and fry for 2-3 minutes, stirring occasionally, until the nuts are golden-brown.

Serve with basmati rice.

Chicken Curries

Chicken Biryani (Serves 6-8)

Ingredients

900g/2lbs chicken (cubed into 4 equal pieces)
560ml/2 1/2 cups of chicken stock
335g/1 1/2 cups of basmati rice
40g/1/4 cup of dried mango pieces
40g/1/4 cup of sultanas
75g/1/2 cup of pistachio nuts (blanched and skinned)
5 whole cloves
2 cinnamon sticks (crushed)
18 green cardamom pods
1 tsp cumin seeds (crushed)
1 tsp coriander seeds (crushed)
handful coriander leaves (chopped)
1 tsp saffron powder
1/2 tsp rock salt
3 cloves of garlic (very finely chopped)
2 inches fresh ginger (peeled and sliced)
5 tbsps ghee
2 onions (sliced)
1 green Serrano chilli (seeded and finely chopped)

Directions

1. Place the chicken stock, chilli pepper, salt, cinnamon, ginger and chicken pieces in a large, heavy saucepan. Bring to the boil. Reduce the heat, cover and simmer for 30 minutes.

2. Remove the chicken and place to one side. Pour the cooked liquid into a large measuring jug and measure to 500ml/2 1/2 cups, adding water if required.

3. Heat the ghee in the saucepan and add the onion. Fry for 3-4 minutes, until golden brown. Remove the onion with a slotted spoon and keep to one side.

4. Add the cloves, cardamom pods and basmati rice to the saucepan and stir-fry for 2-3 minutes.

Chicken Biryani/cont.

5. Add the chicken pieces, followed by the mango, raisins, garlic, pistachios, cumin, saffron and crushed coriander seeds. Cook the mixture for 2-3 minutes, stirring continuously.

6. Pour the stock back into the saucepan and bring to the boil. Reduce the heat, cover and simmer for 13-15 minutes, until the rice is tender and the liquid has been absorbed. Sprinkle the chopped coriander leaves over the top and serve immediately.

Chicken Chettinad (Serves 4-6)

Ingredients

450g/1lb chicken thigh fillets (cut into 1 inch pieces)
4 tomatoes (chopped)
2 cardamom pods (split)
75ml/1/3 cup of buttermilk
3 tbsps vegetable oil
30g/1/8 cup of unsalted butter (softened)
1 tbsp ground coriander
2-3 cloves of garlic (crushed)
1 tbsp crushed black peppercorns
1/2 tsp salt
1/2 inch cinnamon stick
2 cloves
2-3 yellow onions (chopped)
2 tsps chilli powder

2 tsps turmeric
1 tbsp grated fresh ginger
20g/3/4oz fresh coriander leaves (chopped)
8 fresh curry leaves

Directions
1. Place the chicken pieces and buttermilk in a bowl and mix together. Cover and place in the refrigerator for 30 minutes.

2. Mix the vegetable oil and butter together in a bowl.

3. Heat the vegetable oil/butter mixture in a karahi, (or heavy based saucepan). Add the cloves, cardamom and cinnamon and cook, stirring, for about 30 seconds.

4. Add the onions and cook for 8-10 minutes, stirring frequently. Add the garlic and ginger and cook for 1 minute, stirring continuously. Add the salt, turmeric, chilli powder and ground coriander; cook for 1 minute, stirring continuously.

5. Add the tomatoes and cook for 10-12 minutes, until the tomatoes soften.

6. Add the chicken and buttermilk, stirring all the ingredients together well. Cook for 8-10 minutes, stirring frequently.

7. Remove from the heat and stir in the coriander leaves, curry leaves and black pepper.

8. Serve immediately with hot rice.

Chicken Tikka Masala (Serves 6-8)
Ingredients
900g/2lbs chicken breast (cubed)
10 green chillies (chopped)
1 tbsp fried onions
120ml/1/2 cup of plain yoghurt
100ml/1/2 cup of single cream
1/2 lime, juiced

Chicken Tikka Masala/cont.

1/2 tsp garam masala powder
1/2 tbsp ginger paste
1/2 tbsp garlic paste
1/2 tsp salt
handful of coriander (chopped)
1 tbsp butter

Directions

1. Place the green chillies, yoghurt, single cream, lime juice, salt, ginger paste, fried onions, coriander and garlic paste in a food processor and blend until smooth.

2. Transfer to a bowl and add the chicken cubes, tossing and coating the chicken well. Sprinkle the garam masala powder over the top and toss again. Cover and refrigerate overnight (or up to 24 hours).

3. Preheat the oven to 200C/400F/Gas Mark 6.

4. Pour the marinated chicken mixture into a roasting tin and dot evenly over the top with butter.

5. Place in the oven and cook for 15-20 minutes, until cooked. Serve immediately.

Slow-Cook Chicken Curry (Serves 4-6)

Ingredients
4 chicken breasts (skinless and diced)
110ml/1/2 cup of chicken broth
1 onion (chopped)
2 cloves of garlic (crushed)
1/4 tsp cinnamon
1/2 tsp cumin
1/2 tsp turmeric
1/2 tsp crushed red pepper flakes
1/4 ground cardamom
2 tbsps cornstarch
2 tbsps cold water

1 tbsp fresh ginger (grated)
Pinch of ground cloves

Directions

1. To be cooked in a slow cooker. Place the onion, garlic, spices and seasonings in the slow cooker and mix together. Add the diced chicken and pour over the chicken broth.

2. Cover and cook for 6 to 7 hours, until the chicken is cooked through and tender. Transfer the chicken pieces only into a warm serving dish. Keep warm. Increase the slow cooker temperature to high.

3. Mix the cornstarch with the cold water and stir into the cooked liquid. Cook until the sauce thickens, (stir every 5-7 minutes). Once the sauce has thickened pour over the chicken and serve with hot rice.

Chicken Korma (Serves 4)

Ingredients
800g/5 cups diced chicken
1 cup/300ml chicken stock
2 small white onions (finely chopped)
2 tsps ginger puree
2 tsps garlic puree
200g/1 1/2 cups butter ghee
2 tsps turmeric powder
4 tsps mild curry powder
2 tsps garam masala powder
4 egg yolks mixed with 200ml coconut cream
200ml/1 cup single cream
100ml/1/2 cup natural yoghurt
toasted almond slices (to garnish)

Directions

1. Pour the oil into a large saucepan, and bring up to a medium heat. Add the onions and reduce the heat to low. You can optionally add 1 or 2 star anise which help bring out the sweetness. Cook the onions gently and slowly until they turn a golden brown colour.

Chicken Korma/cont.

2. Make a paste of the ginger puree, garlic puree, curry powder and turmeric powder, using a little water. Add to saucepan and stir in well and fry for a couple of minutes.

3. Now add the chicken, and stir in well. Add the coconut cream and egg mixture, and stir well once again.

4. Mix the cream and yoghurt, together in a jug with the chicken stock and pour into the saucepan and mix in well. Turn up the heat until the sauce begins to simmer and leave to simmer for 15-20 minutes. Stir occasionally.

5. Sprinkle in the garam masala and stir in well for the final 2 minutes of cooking. Garnish with the toasted almond slices and serve.

Chicken Vindaloo (Serves 4)

Ingredients

3 cups/600g chopped onions
1 1/2 cups chopped seeded tomatoes (about 4 medium)
2 1/2 tbsps distilled white vinegar
1 large garlic clove (chopped)
1 tsp minced peeled fresh ginger
1 tsp tomato paste
1 tsp garam masala
1 tsp ground turmeric
1/2 tsp paprika
1/2 tsp ground cumin
1/2 tsp ground coriander
1/4 tsp (or more) cayenne pepper
2 tbsps vegetable oil
1 1/2 cups/350ml low-salt chicken broth
6 skinless boneless chicken thighs (cut into 1- to 1 1/2-inch pieces)
1 1/2 lbs/690g russet potatoes (peeled, cut into 1-inch pieces)

Directions

1. Blend the first 11 ingredients and 1/4 teaspoon cayenne pepper in a processor until a paste forms. Heat the oil in heavy large pot over a medium-high heat.

2. Add the paste from processor and cook until golden, stirring occasionally, about 3 minutes. Add chicken and potatoes, then sauté for 5 minutes, whilst stirring intermittently.

3. Add the chicken broth, then bring to boil. Reduce heat to medium-low cover and simmer until potatoes are tender, stirring occasionally, about 15 minutes.

4. Uncover and simmer until chicken is cooked through, about 5 minutes longer.

Season with more cayenne, if desired, and salt and pepper.

Chicken & Spinach Curry (Serves 3-4)

Ingredients
125g/4 1/2 oz basmati rice
1 tbsp vegetable oil
4 skinless chicken breasts
600g/3 cups fresh chicken soup
100g/3 1/2 oz fresh baby spinach

Directions
1. Cook the rice according to packet instructions, then drain.

2. Meanwhile, heat the oil in a deep frying pan over a high heat. Add the chicken and cook for 2-3 minutes each side to brown all over. Pour in the soup and bring back to the boil.

3. Reduce the heat slightly and partially cover the pan with a lid. Simmer for 15 minutes – turning the chicken halfway – or until the chicken is cooked through.

4. Stir the spinach into the sauce, until just wilted. Season, then spoon some rice into bowls, put the chicken on top, then spoon over the sauce. Serve with naan bread.

Chicken Balti (Serves 3-4)

Ingredients

4 chicken breasts (skinned and cut into bite-sized pieces)
2 tbsps ghee
1 red and 1 green sweet pepper (cut into 1/2-inch pieces)
1 medium onion (sliced)
3 red chillies
3 green chillies
1 tsp whole cumin seeds
1 tsp good paprika
1 tsp turmeric
1 tsp garam masala
1/2 tsp ground cinnamon
1 packet curry sauce
1 tsp concentrated tomato purée
salt to taste

Directions

1. Heat a little of the oil in a wok or balti pan over a high heat. Add the peppers and stir fry until they go a little brown at the edges. Remove the peppers from the wok and set aside.

2. Put a little more oil into the wok, heat through, then add some of the chicken pieces and stir fry until they are sealed and have turned white. Remove the chicken from the wok and set aside.

3. Add the rest of the oil to the wok and heat through on a medium heat. Add the onion pieces, chopped chillies and cumin seeds and stir fry until the onion is translucent but not brown.

4. Add the paprika, turmeric and cinnamon, and stir fry for 30 seconds. Return the chicken pieces to the wok along with the curry sauce, tomato purée and salt.

5. Bring to a simmer then cook on a low heat for 30 minutes or until the chicken is cooked. Add a little hot water if the sauce gets too thick.
10 minutes from the end, stir the peppers and garam masala into the sauce. Serve with fresh coriander.

Aromatic Chicken with Raisins (Serves 4)

Ingredients
3 tbsps sunflower oil
6 skinless chicken thighs (on the bone)
1 onion (chopped)
2 bay leaves
4 tbsps rice blend
1 cup/220ml yoghurt
6 stems of fresh coriander leaves (chopped)
1 tbsp curry powder

Directions
1. Heat 1 tbsp of oil in a large pan. Add the chicken and saute for about 7-10 minutes until golden all over, then remove from the pan and keep aside.

2. In the same oil fry the onion until translucent- add more oil if needed. Add bay leaves and the rice blend to the onion and fry for about 5 minutes.

3. Reduce heat to a lower setting and return the chicken to the pan. Mix in the yoghurt, coriander, curry powder together.

4. Add this to the chicken and stir. Cover with the lid and cook on low for 30 minutes, or until the meat falls easily off the bone.

Chicken Dopiaza (Serves 4)

Ingredients
500g/1lb 2oz cubed chicken breast meat
2 tbsps vegetable oil
1 tsp cumin seed
2 large onions, chopped
1 tsp ground turmeric
1 tsp cayenne pepper to taste
1 tsp garam masala
1 clove garlic, crushed
1 tsp minced root ginger
5 tomatoes - peeled, seeded and chopped

Chicken Dopiaza/cont.

Directions

1. Heat oil in a large saucepan over medium heat. Stir in cumin seeds and cook until they start to pop, 20 to 45 seconds.

2. Stir in onion and cook until golden brown, about 5 minutes. Season with turmeric, cayenne, garam masala, garlic and ginger. Cook for 1 to 2 minutes until fragrant.

3. Purée the mixture with the tomatoes in a blender until smooth. Return the purée to the saucepan and add the chicken.

4. Simmer gently until the chicken has cooked, about 20 minutes, add water as needed while cooking to maintain desired consistency.

Chicken Seyal (Serves 6-8)

Ingredients

1 kg/2lb 2oz chicken breasts (cut into pieces)
250g/9oz onions (minced finely)
250g/9oz tomatoes (chopped finely
1/2 cup/110ml of natural yoghurt
1/2 bunch of coriander leaves (chopped)
1/2 bunch of mint leaves (chopped)
100g/4oz spinach leaves (cut finely)
1/2 tsp turmeric powder
1 tsp coriander powder
4 green chillies (minced)
1-inch ginger (minced)
125g/1 cup of ghee
salt and chilli powder to taste

Directions

1. In a large pan, heat the ghee and fry the onions until they start to turn golden. Ensure you keep them moving around the pan.

2. Add the chicken pieces and all the other ingredients one at a time and stir well after adding each ingredient.

3. Cook on a high heat for 5 minutes, then turn down the heat and cook until the chicken is cooked and dry, which should take about 15 minutes.

Serve with poppadoms and basmati rice.

Chicken Madras (Serves 4)

Ingredients
4 skinless, boneless chicken breasts or thighs
1/2 lemon, juiced
1 tsp garam masala
1 tsp salt
2 tbsps ghee
1 large onion (finely chopped)
madras curry paste (1-2 tbsp mild, 3 tbsp medium-hot, and 4-5 tbsp for hot)
400g/16oz can chopped tomatoes
50g/2oz desiccated coconut
small handful of fresh coriander (chopped)

Directions
1. Cut the chicken into bite-size pieces and mix with the lemon juice, and garam masala and season with salt.

2. Heat the ghee in a deep frying pan or saucepan over a medium heat and cook the onion for 6-7 minutes until softened and becoming golden.

3. Add the chicken and fry for 3-4 minutes until it has become opaque in colour. Stir in the madras paste and cook for a couple of minutes before adding the chopped tomatoes and coconut.

4. Cover with a lid and leave to simmer gently for about 20 minutes. Stir in the chopped coriander and serve straight away with naan bread.

Leftover Chicken Biryani (Serves 6)

Ingredients

400g/14oz cooked, skinless chicken diced
2 tbsps sunflower oil
4 carrots, diced
2 red onions, sliced
600g/3 cups basmati rice
1.2 litres hot chicken stock
2 tbsps madras curry paste
4 tsps fresh coriander, roughly chopped

Directions

1. Add the oil to a large flameproof casserole dish and set it over a medium heat. Add the carrots and onions, and cook for 5-6 minutes until the onions are softened. Add the rice, pour over the stock, then add the turkey.

2. Stir in the curry paste and bring to the boil. Reduce the heat then cover and simmer gently for about 15 minutes, until the rice is tender and the liquid has been absorbed.

3. Stir in the coriander, then divide between serving bowls. Serve with poppadoms and chutney.

Vegetable Curries

Black Bean Curry (Serves 4)

Ingredients

500g/1lb 2oz black beans (soaked overnight and drained)
395g/1 3/4 cups of chopped, canned tomatoes
3 celery sticks (chopped)
2 onions (sliced)
4 cloves of garlic (crushed)
1 tsp chilli powder
1 cm piece of root ginger (finely chopped)
2 tsps ground cumin
2 tsps ground coriander
1 tsp cardamom seeds
1 tsp chilli powder
3 tbsps vegetable oil
1 tsp garam masala
1 tbsp fresh coriander leaves (chopped)
salt (to season)

Directions

1. Place the drained beans in a pan and cover with cold water. Bring to the boil and boil rapidly for 10 minutes. Reduce the heat, cover and simmer for 1-1 1/2 hours, until tender. Add a pinch of salt towards the end of the cooking time. Drain the beans, reserving 300ml/1/2 pint of the liquid.

2. Heat the vegetable oil in a saucepan and add the onions, cook for 3-4 minutes, until softened. Stir in the garam masala, cumin, ground coriander, chilli powder, ginger, garlic and cook for 1 minute, stirring continuously.

3. Add the reserved liquid to the saucepan, followed by the chopped tomatoes, beans, celery and cardamom seeds. Season with salt, according to taste. Bring to the boil and then reduce the heat, cover and simmer for 40-45 minutes.

4. Remove from the heat and stir in the chopped coriander leaves. Serve immediately with hot rice.

Mixed Vegetable Curry (Serves 6)

Ingredients

250g/9oz potatoes (diced)
125g/4 1/2 oz sweet potatoes (diced)
160g/1/2 cup of cauliflower florets
1 small courgette (diced)
4-5 carrots (diced)
180g/1 cup of green beans (sliced)
1 onion (sliced)
4 tomatoes (skinless and chopped)
1 tsp turmeric
2 tsps ground coriander
1 tsp ground cumin
1 tsp chilli powder
375ml/1 2/3 cups of vegetable stock
3 tbsps vegetable oil

Directions

1. Heat the vegetable oil in a large saucepan and add the onion. Cook for 4-5 minutes, until tender. Add the chilli powder, coriander, cumin and turmeric, cooking for 2-3 minutes and stirring frequently.

2. Add the cauliflower florets, sweet potatoes, potatoes, carrots and green beans, coating them well with the spices.

3. Add the chopped tomatoes and vegetable stock and bring to the boil. Reduce the heat and simmer for 10-13 minutes, until the vegetables are tender.

4. Serve immediately with hot rice.

Dry Potato Curry (Serves 4-6)

Ingredients

650g/1lb 7oz waxy potatoes (cut into 2cm chunks)
1 large onion (finely sliced)
1 tsp cumin
1 tsp turmeric
1 tsp cayenne pepper

1 tsp mustard seeds
2 cloves of garlic (crushed)
1 inch piece of fresh root ginger (grated)
1 fresh green chilli (deseeded and chopped)
2 tbsps vegetable oil

Directions
1. Boil the potatoes for 7-8 minutes, until just tender – drain and set aside.

2. Heat the vegetable oil in a large saucepan and add the mustard seeds then cook for 30-40 seconds, until they begin to pop. Add the onion and cook for 4-5 minutes, until tender.

3. Stir in the ginger and garlic and cook for 1 minute. Add the chilli, turmeric, cumin, cayenne pepper and potato chunks and combine well. Cover the saucepan and cook for 4-5 minutes, stirring occasionally.

4. Once the potatoes are tender and flavoured well with spices. Transfer to a serving dish and serve immediately.

Spinach and Paneer Curry (Serves 6)

Ingredients
300g/11oz paneer (cut into 2cm cubes) *
180ml/3/4 cup single cream
1kg/2 1/4 lbs baby spinach leaves
5 cloves of garlic (finely chopped)
2 inch piece of fresh root ginger (finely chopped)
1 tsp garam masala
1 1/2 tsps chilli flakes
1 tsp cumin seeds
70ml/1/3 cup vegetable oil

Directions
1. Heat the vegetable oil in a large saucepan and add the chilli flakes and cumin seeds. Cook over a medium/high heat for 30-40 seconds.

Spinach and Paneer Curry/cont.

2. Reduce the heat and add the ginger and garlic; cook for 10-20 seconds. Add the spinach and garam masala; mixing the ingredients together well. Cook for 8-10 minutes, until the leaves have cooked and softened. Remove from the heat.

3. Transfer the contents of the saucepan into a food processor, (including the juices), and blend into a smooth paste. Return to the saucepan and reheat.

4. Pour in the cream and combine well. Add the paneer and cook for a couple of minutes, until warmed through. Serve immediately.

* Paneer is an Indian cheese.

Vegetable Biryani (Serves 4)

Ingredients

65g/2 1/2oz red lentils (rinsed)
1 large carrot (diced)
225g/9oz cauliflower (cut into florets)
100g/4oz frozen peas
1 onion (chopped)
65g/2 1/2oz sultanas
200g/8oz basmati rice (rinsed)
5 cardamom pods (split)
5 cloves
1 tsp ground turmeric
1 tsp cumin seeds
1 bay leaf
1 cinnamon stick (broken in 2)
1 tbsp fresh coriander leaves (chopped)
600ml/2 1/2 cups vegetable stock
salt and black pepper (to season)

Directions

1. Place the spices, bay leaf, cauliflower, onion, rice, lentils, peas, carrot and sultanas in a large saucepan. Season with salt and black pepper, according to taste.

2. Pour the stock into the saucepan and bring to the boil. Reduce the heat a little, cover and simmer for 20 minutes, stirring occasionally.

3. Remove from the heat and leave to stand for 10 minutes, until the stock has been absorbed by the rice. Remove the cardamom pods, cinnamon stick, cloves and bay leaf.

4. Gently fluff the rice with a fork and sprinkle over the top with chopped coriander leaves.

Serve immediately.

Coconut & Potato Shakuti (Serves 2-4)

Curry paste ingredients
2 tsps vegetable oil
3 cloves
1/2 cinnamon stick
2 tsp poppy seeds
1/2 tsp black peppercorns
4 dry red chillies or 1 tsp red chilli flakes
75g/2 1/2 oz grated desiccated coconut
4 garlic cloves
2 medium onions

Curry ingredients
4 tsps vegetable oil
4 medium potatoes, chopped into 2.5cm/1in cubes
1 tin chopped tomatoes
200g/7 1/2 oz boiled green peas
1 tsp salt

Directions
1. To make the curry paste, heat the oil in a pan. Fry the cloves, cinnamon, poppy seeds, peppercorns and red chillies for one minute.

2. Dry roast the coconut in a separate pan until it is golden brown. Place the fried spices, coconut, garlic cloves and onions in a blender and grind to paste.

3. To make the curry, heat the oil in a pan and add the diced potatoes. Cover and cook for two minutes.

4. Next add the paste, chopped tomatoes, peas and salt. Stir, cover and simmer for ten minutes until the potatoes are cooked through.

Mushroom & Potato Curry (Serves 4)

Ingredients
1 tbsp olive oil
1 onion (roughly chopped)
1 large potato (chopped into small chunks)
1 aubergine (trimmed and chopped into chunks)
250g/9oz button mushrooms
2-4 tbsps curry paste (depending on how spicy you want it)
150ml/2/3 cup vegetable stock
400ml/1 3/4 cups reduced-fat coconut milk
chopped coriander (to serve)

Directions
1. Heat the oil in a large saucepan, then add the onion and potato. Cover, then cook over a low heat for 5 minutes until the potatoes start to soften. Throw in the aubergine and mushrooms, then cook for a few more minutes.

2. Stir in the curry paste, pour over the stock and coconut milk. Bring to the boil, then simmer for 10 minutes or until the potato is tender. Stir through the coriander.

Serve with rice and naan bread.

Vegetable Pullao (Serves 2)

Ingredients

Basmati rice (measured to the 450ml/ 3/4-pint level in a measuring jug)
3 tbsps olive oil
1/2 tsp brown mustard seeds
1 hot green chilli (finely chopped)
100g/4oz potato (peeled and chopped)
2/3 carrot (peeled and cut into 5mm dice)
40g/1 1/2 oz green beans (cut into 5mm segments)
1/2 tsp ground turmeric
1 tsp garam masala
1 tsp very finely grated fresh root ginger
1 tsp salt
570ml/1 pint water

Directions

1. Wash the rice in several changes of water then drain. Put it in a bowl, cover with water and leave to soak for 30 minutes, then drain again.

2. Put the oil in a heavy-based pan (with a tight-fitting lid) and set it over a medium high heat. When it is hot, put in the mustard seeds. As soon as they begin to pop, put in the chilli, potato, carrot, green beans, turmeric, garam masala and ginger. Sauté, stirring for 1 minute.

4. Reduce the heat to medium-low and add the drained rice and the salt. Cook the rice gently, stirring for 2 minutes.

4. Add the water and bring to the boil. Cover the pan tightly with a close-fitting lid or with foil and a lid, then turn the heat to very low and cook for 25 minutes.

Mango Curry (Serves 4-6)

Ingredients

3 medium ripe mangoes (peeled, pith removed and chopped)
1 tsp ground turmeric
1 tsp cayenne pepper
1-1 1/2 tsps salt
55g/2oz brown sugar (optional)

310g/11oz coconut (freshly grated)
3-4 fresh hot green chillies (coarsley chopped)
1/2 tbsp cumin seeds
290ml/1/2 pint natural yoghurt (lightly beaten)
2 tbsps coconut oil
1/2 tsp brown mustard seeds
3-4 dried hot red chillies (broken into halves)
1/2 tsp fenugreek seeds
10-12 fresh curry leaves

Directions

1. Put the mangoes in a medium-sized pan. Add 250ml/9fl oz water. Cover and stew for 8-10 minutes over a meduim-low heat. Stir occasionally.

2. Add the turmeric, cayenne pepper and salt. Stir well. (If the mangoes are not sweet enough, add brown sugar to make the dish sweeter.)

3. Meanwhile, put the coconut, green chillies and cumin seeds into a blender. Add 250ml/9fl oz water and blend to a fine paste.

4. When the mangoes are cooked, mash them to a pulp. Add the coconut paste. Mix. Cover and simmer over a medium heat, stirring occasionally, until the mixture becomes thick. This should take about 10-15 minutes.

5. Add the yoghurt and heat, stirring, until just warmed through. Do not let the mixture come to the boil. Remove from the heat and put to one side. Check for seasoning.

6. Heat the oil in a small pan over a medium-high heat. When hot, add the mustard seeds. When the mustard seeds begin to pop (a matter of a few seconds) add the chillies, fenugreek seeds and the curry leaves.

7. Stir fry for a few seconds until the chillies darken. Quickly add the contents of the small pan to the mangoes.

Stir to mix, and then serve.

Vegetable & Cashew Biryani (Serves 6)

Ingredients

500g/1lb 2oz basmati rice
2 large onions (halved and thinly sliced)
4 tbsps sunflower oil
large piece fresh root ginger (shredded)
65g/1/4 cup korma curry paste
2 cinnamon sticks
6 green cardamom pods
3 star anise
250g/9oz diced potatoes
1 small cauliflower (cut into small florets)
250g/9oz Greek yoghurt
225g/8oz frozen peas
2 good pinches saffron
1/2 tsp rosewater
butter (for greasing)
100g/3 1/2oz roasted or salted cashew nuts

Directions

1. Rinse the rice in several changes of water to remove excess starch, then put in a bowl of cold water and leave to soak for 30 minutes.

2. Meanwhile, fry the onions in the oil for 8 minutes until soft and starting to colour. Add the ginger, then cook for 2 minutes more. Stir in the curry paste followed by the whole spices, cook for 1 minute more, then tip in the potatoes and cauliflower.

3. Pour in 300ml/1 1/3 cup water, cover and boil for about 5-7 minutes until the vegetables are just tender, but still have a little resistance. Stir in the yoghurt and peas with 1 tsp salt.

4. Mix the saffron, rosewater and 3 tbsp boiling water together and stir well. Drain the rice, tip into a pan of boiling salted water, then cook for 5 minutes until almost tender, then drain again.

5. Get out a large ovenproof dish with a lid and butter the base. Tip the curry sauce into the base, scatter over the nuts, then spoon over the rice. Drizzle over the rosewater mixture, then cover with foil followed by the lid. Can be chilled overnight until ready to cook.

6. Heat oven to 180C/350F/Gas Mark 4. Put the biryani in the oven for 45 minutes-1 hour until thoroughly heated through. To check it's ready, try a spoonful from the centre of the rice.

Pumpkin Curry with Chickpeas (Serves 4)

Ingredients
1 tbsp sunflower oil
3 tbsps curry paste
2 onions (finely chopped)
6 cardamom pods
1 tbsp mustard seed
1 piece pumpkin
250ml/1 1/4 cup vegetable stock
400ml/1 3/4 cups reduced-fat coconut milk
400g/15oz tin chickpeas, drained and rinsed
2 limes
large handful mint leaves

Directions
1. Heat the oil in a sauté pan, then gently fry the curry paste with the onions, lemongrass, cardamom and mustard seed for 2-3 minutes until fragrant.

2. Stir the pumpkin or squash into the pan and coat in the paste, then pour in the stock and coconut milk.

3. Bring everything to a simmer, add the chickpeas, then cook for about 10 minutes until the pumpkin is tender. The curry can now be cooled and frozen for up to 1 month.

4. Squeeze the juice of one lime into the curry, then cut the other lime into wedges to serve alongside.

5. Just before serving, tear over mint leaves, then bring to the table with the lime wedges and warm naan bread.

Spicy Vegetable & Quinoa Curry (Serves 4)

Ingredients
1 onion (sliced)
4 tbsps vegetarian korma curry paste
1ltr/4 1/4 cups milk
750g/2lbs 9oz frozen mixed vegetables
175g/6 1/2oz quinoa (rinsed)

Directions
1. Simmer the onion and the curry paste with a splash of water for 5 minutes in a large saucepan, stirring from time to time.

2. Heat the milk in a jug in the microwave. Add the vegetables and quinoa, then stir in the milk.

3. Bring to the boil, simmer gently for 10 mins until the quinoa is cooked. Check seasoning. Serve with warm naan bread.

Pumpkin, Spinach & Black Bean Dopiaza (Serves 2)

Ingredients
2 onions (thinly sliced)
2 tbsps sunflower oil
1 garlic clove (crushed)
1 tsp each ground cumin, coriander and curry powder
pinch chilli powder
400g/14oz pumpkin (peeled weight and then cut into chunks)
1 tbsp tomato purée
400g/14oz can black beans in water (drained and rinsed)
200g/7oz spinach (washed)

Directions
1. Heat oven to 190C/375F/Gas Mark 5. Toss half the onions in 1 tbsp oil, then roast for 15-20 minutes, until they are crisp and golden.

2. Meanwhile, fry the remaining onion in the oil until lightly golden. Add the garlic and spices, cook for 1 minute. Add the pumpkin, stir in the tomato purée and 425ml/3/4 pint boiling water, then return to the boil.

3. Simmer, covered, for 15 minutes, then stir in the beans. Cook for a further 5 minutes. Put the spinach in a colander and pour over a kettle of boiling water until it is wilted. Press with a wooden spoon to remove excess water, then roughly chop.

4. Stir into the curry, then warm through. Serve scattered with the crisp roasted onions.

Pea & Tomato Curry (Serves 4)

Ingredients
250g/9oz paneer (indian cheese) cut into chunks
4 very ripe tomatoes (roughly chopped)
1 onion (blended to a purée with a piece of ginger and clove of garlic)
300g/1 1/2 cups frozen peas (defrosted)
300ml/1 1/2 cups vegetable stock
2 tbsps olive oil

Ingredients for spice mix
2 tsps garam masala
1/2 tsp turmeric
pinch of cayenne

Directions
1. Fry the paneer in 2 tbsps of oil until golden brown, then scoop out. Fry the onion mix until fragrant, about 5 minutes.

2. Stir in the spices, then the tomatoes and stock, and simmer for 10 minutes until thickened. Add the paneer and peas and cook for 5 extra minutes, and then serve.

Herb & Almond Pilaf (Serves 4)

Ingredients

50g/2oz butter (plus a little extra)
2 large onions (halved and sliced)
2 garlic cloves (sliced)
1 cinnamon stick
4 cloves
5 cardamom pods (bruised)
300g/11oz basmati rice
550ml/2 1/2 cups vegetable stock
2 tbsps olive oil (for deep frying)
4 tbsps blanched almonds
1 tbsp parsley
1 tbsp chive
1 tbsp coriander

Directions

1. Melt 50g/2oz butter in a large, wide pan and cook half the onions and all the garlic until soft and golden.

2, Add the spices and cook for a couple of minutes. Add the basmati and stir until coated. Pour in the stock. Turn the heat down to a simmer then cover and cook for 10-15 minutes until all the stock has been absorbed and the rice is tender.

3. Meanwhile, heat a 2cm-layer of oil in a pan and deep-fry the remaining onions until crisp. In a separate pan fry the almonds in a little more butter until golden. Stir the herbs into the pilaf and scatter the almonds and crisp onions over.

Paneer & Tomato Curry (Serves 4)

Ingredients

1/2 tsp cumin seeds
1 green chilli (chopped and seeded)
3cm piece of fresh root ginger (peeled and chopped)
150g/5 1/2 oz Greek yoghurt
1 tsp light muscovado sugar

1/2 tsp garam masala
2 tbsps chopped fresh coriander leaves and stems
1/2 lime, juiced
3 tbsps tomato purée
250g/9oz frozen peas
225g/8oz pack paneer (cut into 1cm cubes)
2-3 firm red tomatoes (cut into wedges)
a handful of roasted cashew nuts (chopped to serve)

Directions
1. Toast the cumin seeds in a heavy pan to darken - about 30 seconds. Crush roughly with a rolling pin, then tip into a blender with the chilli, ginger, yoghurt, sugar, garam masala, coriander, lime juice, tomato purée and 200ml/7fl oz water, then blend until smooth.

2. Pour the sauce into a saucepan. Cook for 5 minutes, stirring often. Add the peas and simmer for 3-5 minutes until almost cooked.

3. Stir in the paneer and tomato and heat through for 2-3 minutes. Scatter with cashews.

Spicy Okra Curry (Serves 4)
Ingredients
5 tbsps olive oil
400g/15oz onions (sliced)
500g/1lb 2oz okra (trimmed, washed, dried and sliced into 2cm pieces)
2 tomatoes (diced)
1 red chilli (finely chopped - or 1/2 tsp powdered)
2 tsps ground coriander
handful fresh coriander (roughly chopped, to serve)

Directions
1. Heat a large wok or frying pan over a medium heat. Add the oil, then the onions, cooking until soft. Stir in the okra. Add the tomatoes and chilli, then season. Mix well and keep stirring gently, taking care not to break up the okra.

Spicy Okra Curry/cont.

2. Okra releases a sticky substance when cooked, but keep cooking, stirring gently - this will disappear and the tomatoes will become pulpy, after about 10 minutes.

3. Lower the heat, add the ground coriander and cook for another 5-10 minutes. Add 2 tbsps of water, cover and let simmer for another 4-5 minutes.

Sprinkle with coriander and serve with basmati rice or chapati bread.

Rice & Breads

Naan Bread (Makes 5-6)

Ingredients
460g/4 cups of unbleached white flour
25g/1oz fresh yeast
1 tsp salt
2 eggs
4 tbsps natural yoghurt
120ml/1/2 cup milk (at room temperature)
5 tbsps butter
2 tbsps vegetable oil

Directions
1. Sift the flour and salt into a large bowl and mix together. Place the yeast and milk in a separate bowl and cream together. Set aside for 20 minutes.

2. Add the yeast mixture, eggs, yoghurt and vegetable oil to the flour/salt and combine well. Mix into a soft dough.

3. Lightly flour a clean work surface and turn out the dough. Knead the dough for 8-10 minutes, until smooth. Return to the bowl, cover and set aside for 50-60 minutes, until it has increased in size by about double.

4. Preheat the oven to 230C/450F/Gas mark 8. Turn the dough back out onto a lightly floured work surface and knead for 2-3 minutes.

Naan Bread/cont.

5. Divide the dough into 5-6 pieces, shaped into ball shapes. Roll out each of the balls into a teardrop-shape, about 23cm long, 12cm wide and 1/4 inch thick.

6. Place the naan breads onto preheated baking trays and place in the oven for 4-5 minutes, until risen.

7. Whilst the breads are baking, preheat the grill to a high heat.

8. Remove the naan breads from the oven and place under the grill for about 30 seconds each side, until lightly browned.

9. Brush with butter and serve immediately with curry of your choice.

Punjabi Missi Rotis (Makes 8)

Ingredients
140g/1 1/4 cups of gram flour (also known as chickpea/besan flour)
140g/1 1/4 cups of wholemeal flour
1 onion (finely chopped)
2 fresh green chillies (deseeded and finely chopped)
1 tsp ground turmeric
1 tsp salt
1 1/2 tbsps fresh coriander leaves (chopped)
240-280ml/1 1/4 cups of water (at room temperature)
4-6 tbsps unsalted butter (melted)

Directions
1. Place the besan and wholemeal flour in a large bowl and add the onion, coriander, turmeric, salt and chilli. Combine well. Stir in 2 tbsps of melted butter.

2. Gradually add water to make a soft dough. Lightly flour a clean work surface and turn out the dough. Knead for 8-10 minutes, until smooth.

3. Lightly grease a bowl with vegetable oil and place the dough inside. Cover with cling wrap and set aside for 30-40 minutes.

4. Preheat the oven to a low setting.

5. Turn the dough back onto the lightly floured surface and divide into 8 equal-sized pieces. Roll into balls and then using a rolling pin, roll out each ball into a 1cm thick round, 16-18cm in diameter.

6. Heat a frying pan and brush both sides of a roti with melted butter. Carefully drop into the frying pan and cook for 1 minute. Turn the rotis over and cook for 1 minute.

7. Remove from the frying pan and brush lightly with a little more melted butter. Transfer to plate and save in the oven. Repeat this process for the remaining rotis. Serve hot!

Sweet Saffron Rice (Serves 4-6)

Ingredients
250g/1 cup of basmati rice (rinsed)
150g/1 cup of raisins
8 cardamom pods (bruised)
8 cloves
1 1/2 tsps saffron threads
4 1/2 tbsps boiling water
4 tbsps vegetable oil
1 x 3 inch cinnamon stick
4 tbsps sugar
salt (to season)

Directions
1. Place the rice in a large bowl and cover with cold water. Soak for 30 minutes. Once soaked, drain the rice, reserving the water.

2. Place the saffron threads in a small bowl and add the boiling water then soak for 5 minutes.

3. Heat the vegetable oil in a large saucepan and add the cinnamon, cardamom pods and cloves. Fry for 1 minute.

Sweet Saffron Rice/cont.

4. Add the soaked rice to the saucepan and cook for 3-4 minutes, until golden. Add the reserved rice water, saffron, (including the soaking water), sugar and raisins. Season with salt, according to taste. Bring to the boil.

5. Reduce the heat, cover and simmer for 13-15 minutes, stirring occasionally, until the water is absorbed and the rice is cooked. Remove the spices.

Serve immediately.

Yellow Aromatic Basmati Rice (Serves 4-6)

Ingredients
250g/2 cups of basmati rice (rinsed)
1 onion (chopped)
2 cloves of garlic (finely chopped)
450ml/2 cups of hot chicken stock
6 green cardamoms (crushed)
110g/4oz slivered almonds
50g/2/3 cup of sultanas
3 tbsps vegetable oil
2-3 drops of yellow food colouring
handful of fresh coriander leaves (chopped)
salt and black pepper (to season)

Directions
1. Place the rinsed basmati rice in a bowl and cover with cold water. Leave to soak for 30 minutes. Drain and stand for a further 2-3 minutes.

2. Heat 2 tbsps of the vegetable oil in a large saucepan and add the garlic and onion. Cook for 4-5 minutes, until tender.

3. Add the rice to the saucepan and cook for 2-3 minutes, stirring continuously. Add the cardamoms and season with salt and black pepper.

4. Pour in enough stock to just cover the rice and bring to the boil, without stirring. Reduce the heat, cover and simmer for 10 minutes.

5. Whilst the rice is simmering, heat the remaining vegetable oil in a saucepan and add the almond slivers. Cook for 2-3 minutes, stirring continuously, until golden brown. Remove the almonds with a slotted spoon and drain on paper kitchen towel. Set aside.

6. Drop a few drops of the food colouring into the rice, without stirring it in. Re-cover and simmer for a further 5 minutes.

7. Add the sultanas and almonds to the rice and gently mix into the rice. Re-cover, remove from the heat and stand for 5 minutes. Transfer to a dish and serve immediately.

Spinach and Pea Pilau Rice (Serves 2)

Ingredients
250g/2 cups basmati rice
1 cinnamon stick (halved)
8 green cardamom pods
6 cloves
2 tsps cumin seeds
100g/4oz fresh baby spinach (roughly shredded)
200g/8oz frozen peas

Directions
1. Thoroughly rinse the rice in a bowl or sieve with several changes of water until the water runs clear. Drain well, then heat a large pan on the stove, tip in the spices, then dry-fry for about 1 minute until they are toasted (not burnt) and beginning to release their aromas.

2. Tip the rice into the pan, stir well over the heat, then pour in 4 mugs of water and add 1 tsp of salt.

3. Bring to the boil, then cover and simmer for 8 mins until the rice is almost tender and the water has been absorbed.

4. Stir in the spinach and peas, then cover and leave for 2 minutes so the peas defrost and the spinach just wilts.

Pilau Rice

Ingredients

1 tbsp groundnut oil
1 small onion (finely chopped)
1 cinnamon stick (split lengthways)
3/4 tsp cumin seeds (dry-toasted in a pan and crushed)
2 cardamom pods
6 cloves
2 tsps ground turmeric
few sprigs fresh thyme
2 bay leaves
250g/2 cups long grain rice

Directions

1. Heat the oil in a large pan with a tight-fitting lid. Add the onion and gently cook until softened. Stir in the spices and herbs and cook for 1 minute.

2. Add the rice and stir until coated. Add 600ml/2 2/3 cups boiling water and bring to the boil. Cover, then simmer on the lowest setting for 12-15 minutes, until tender.

3. Let the steam dry off, then fluff up with a fork.

Naan Bread Dippers and Mint Raita (Serves 6)

Ingredients

4-6 naan breads (cut into strips)
1 tbsp lemon juice
1/2 cucumber (grated)
500g/2 cups of Greek yoghurt
1 1/2-2 handfuls of fresh coriander leaves
handful of fresh mint leaves
3 tbsps olive oil
paprika (to season)
salt and black pepper (to season)

Directions

1. Place the grated cucumber in a bowl and squeeze out as much juice as you can, using your hands. Remove the juice, leaving the grated cucumber.

2. Place the mint and coriander leaves and Greek yoghurt in a food processor and blend until well combined. Transfer to a dish.

3. Stir the cucumber into the mixture; mixing together well. Cover and refrigerate for at least 20 minutes.

4. Preheat the oven to 180C/350F/Gas mark 4.

5. Lay the naan strips on baking trays and brush the top side with the olive oil. Sprinkle over the top with salt, black pepper and paprika.

6. Place in the oven for 7-10 minutes, until crisp and lightly browned. Remove from the oven and leave to cool for 1-2 minutes.

7. Add the lemon juice to the Raita and serve with the naan dippers.

Spiced Basmati Rice (Serves 4-6)

Ingredients

300g/1 1/3 cup of basmati rice (rinsed)
2 black cardamoms
1 inch stick of cinnamon
4 cloves
2 bay leaves
1/2 tsp cumin seeds
2 tbsps vegetable oil
1/2 tsp salt

Directions

1. Place the rinsed basmati rice in a bowl and cover with cold water. Leave to soak for 30 minutes. Drain and stand for a further 2-3 minutes.

2. Heat the vegetable oil in a saucepan and add the cardamoms, cumin seeds, cloves, cinnamon and bay leaves. Cook for 2-3 minutes, stirring continuously.

3. Add the rice and sprinkle over with salt; stir into the spice mixture, coating the rice well.

4. Cover the rice with water – coming to about 1 inch above the rice. Bring to the boil. Reduce the heat, cover and simmer for 20 minutes; until the rice is cooked and all the water has been absorbed.

5. Remove from the heat and fluff the rice with a fork. Adjust seasoning, if required. Transfer into a dish and serve immediately.

Crispy Poppadoms & Tomato Chutney (Serves 2)

Ingredients for Crispy Poppadoms
300ml/1/2 pint vegetable oil, for deep frying
3 raw poppadoms

Ingredients for Tomato Chutney
dash olive oil
1/2 onion, peeled, finely chopped
1 garlic clove, finely chopped
1 fresh tomato, chopped
1 tsp soft brown sugar
pinch chilli flakes
2 tsps red wine vinegar
1 tbsp each chopped fresh basil, mint and coriander
salt and freshly ground black pepper

Crispy Poppadoms & Tomato Chutney/cont.

Directions

1. For the crisp poppadoms, pour the oil into a large saucepan or deep fat fryer and heat until a small cube of bread turns golden in 30 seconds.

2. Carefully lower the poppadums into the hot oil and fry for 30 seconds or until crisp. Remove with a slotted spoon and drain on kitchen papers.

3. For the tomato chutney, heat the olive oil in a small saucepan, add the onion and fry gently for four minutes or until softened. Add the garlic and fry for one minute.

4. Add the chopped tomato, brown sugar, chilli and red wine vinegar and simmer for 4-5 minutes. Stir in the herbs and season well with salt and freshly ground black pepper.

Serve the chutney in a dipping bowl alongside the poppadoms.

Peshwari Naan Bread (Makes 2)

Ingredients
250g/8 1/2 oz plain flour (plus extra for dusting)
2 tsps sugar
1/2 tsp salt
1/2 tsp baking powder
110-130ml/4 1/2 fl oz milk
30g/1oz flaked almonds
1 tbsp butter (melted, for serving)

Filling Ingredients
70g/2 1/2 oz pistachios, shells removed
35g/1 1/4 oz raisins
1 1/2 tsps caster sugar

Directions

1. Sift together the flour, sugar, salt and baking powder in a bowl. Mix the milk and oil together in a separate bowl. Make a well in the centre of the dry ingredients and pour in the liquid ingredients.

2. Slowly mix together the dough by working from the centre and use the flour from the edges of the well until you have a smooth, soft dough. Knead for 8-10 minutes, adding a little flour if the dough is too sticky.

3. Place in an oiled bowl, cover with a damp tea-towel and leave in a warm place for at least an hour, until the dough has doubled in size. Then knock back and form into five equal-sized balls.

4. For the filling, pulse together the pistachios, raisins and sugar in a food processor until the mixture forms a coarse powder. Divide into five equal portions.

5. Preheat the grill to its highest setting and place a heavy baking sheet on the top shelf to heat.

6. Roll out each of the five portions of dough balls into thick circles. Fill half of each circle with one portion of the filling leaving about a one-inch margin around the edge.

7. Wet the dough around the edges with a little water and fold each circle in half to enclose the filling. Pinch the dough around the edges to close.

8. Gently roll out each naan into a teardrop or oval shape. Sprinkle over the flaked almonds. Place the naan on the hot baking sheet and grill for about 1-2 minutes until there are nice brown spots on the surface.

Brush with the melted butter and serve hot as an accompaniment to a curry.

Chapati (Serves 4)

Ingredients
115g/1 cup of wheat flour (can use wholemeal flour)
1/2 tsp salt
1 tsp ghee
warm water

Directions
1. Prepare the dough by mixing together 110ml/1/2 cup of water with 1/2 tsp salt, 1 tsp ghee and just enough wheat flour. Knead well. Put to one side for about 45 minutes.

2. Take some dough and make small balls - about the size of a golf ball. Dust with wheat flour and roll into chapatis on a rolling board.

3. Heat an ungreased skillet over a medium heat, place the chapati into the skillet and let cook for about 1 minute. Turn and cook the second side for 2/3 minute till small bubbles form.

4. Turn again and cook the first side - it should puff. Serve warm. Add more ghee on top of chapati if wanted.

Turmeric Pilau Rice with Golden Onions (Serves 2)

Ingredients
400g/14oz basmati rice
4 tbsps olive oil
1 1/2 tsps cumin seeds
1 tsp black mustard seeds
2 large onions (halved and sliced)
1 tsp tumeric
2 red or green chillies (deseeded and thinly sliced)

Directions
1. Thoroughly rinse the rice until the water looks completely clear. Drain, then tip into a large pan of salted water.

2. Bring to the boil and cook for 6 mins until just tender, but check after 5 minutes. Drain well, cool and chill.

3. Heat the oil in a large wok and fry the spices until they start to pop. Add the onions, then cook, stirring frequently, until the onions are tender and golden.

4. Stir in the turmeric and chilli, and cook for 1-2 minutes more. Allow to cool before serving.

Potato Parantha (Serves 4)

Ingredients
250g/2 cups wheat flour
2 medium potatoes (boiled, peeled, mashed and cooled to room temperature)
1 tsp coriander powder
1 tsp cumin powder
1/2 tsp amchoor powder/mango powder
1 green chilli minced (optional)
1 tsp chilli powder
1 tsp lime/lemon juice
salt to taste
finely chopped coriander

Directions
1. Mix mashed potatoes, coriander powder, cumin powder, mango powder, chopped green chilies, salt, coriander, lime juice and chilli powder.

2. Make small balls of the mixture. Take a ball of dough, about the size of a large egg size or peach, and roll it to a circle 4-5 inches in diameter.

Potato Parantha/cont.

3. Place the potato mixture on the dough and again make it into a ball. Seal the edges completely so that the potato mix doesn't come out.

4. Flatten with the plam heel of your hand, then roll into a 6 inch circle. Pre-heat the griddle. Turn it and coat with a little oil or butter and cook over low heat.

5. Turn it again and spread butter/oil on the other side. Cook both sides till golden brown.

Serve with chutney, yogurt, steamed vegetable and pickles.

Raitas & Chutneys

Coconut Chutney

Ingredients

115g/4oz coconut (freshly grated)
110g/4oz chopped, fresh green coriander
1 small onion or 2 shallots (peeled and coarsely chopped)
2.5cm/1-inch piece of fresh ginger (peeled and coarsely chopped)
2 garlic cloves (peeled and coarsely chopped)
2 tbsps lemon juice
1 tsp coriander seeds
2 cloves
1cm/1/2-inch piece of cinnamon stick
1 tsp salt
1 tsp sugar

Directions

1. Put the coconut, coriander, onion or shallot, ginger, garlic, chillies and lemon juice in a food processor. Blend, adding 4 tbsps of water as needed to get a thick, coarse paste.

2. Put the coriander seeds, cloves and cinnamon into a clean coffee grinder and grind them to a fine powder. Mix the powder with the coconut mixture. Add the salt and sugar.

3. Stir to mix and taste for the blend of sweet and sour. Cover and refrigerate until needed.

Raitas & Chutneys

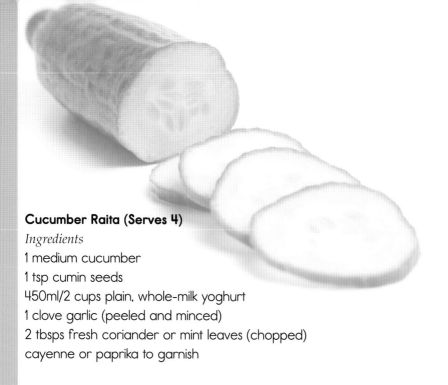

Cucumber Raita (Serves 4)

Ingredients
1 medium cucumber
1 tsp cumin seeds
450ml/2 cups plain, whole-milk yoghurt
1 clove garlic (peeled and minced)
2 tbsps fresh coriander or mint leaves (chopped)
cayenne or paprika to garnish

Directions
1. Peel the cucumber. Cut lengthwise into 1/4-inch strips, then into thin slices crosswise. Blot off moisture with paper towels. Toast cumin seeds for a few seconds in a small, heavy frying pan over high heat.

2. In a bowl, stir the yoghurt until it is smooth. Mix it with the cumin, garlic and coriander or mint leaves. Combine mixture with cucumber slivers, sprinkle with cayenne or paprika, and chill before serving.

Cucumber and Mint Raita

Ingredients
250g/1 cup of natural yoghurt
2 tbsps fresh mint (chopped)
1/2 tsp ground cumin
pinch of cayenne pepper
1 cucumber (peeled and finely diced)

Directions
1. Place all of the ingredients in a bowl and mix together well. Transfer to a serving dish. Cover and refrigerate for 1 hour before serving.

Pomegranate Raita

Ingredients
1 small pomegranate
450ml/2 cups plain, whole-milk yoghurt
handful of chopped fresh coriander leaves and stalks
salt and freshly ground black pepper, to taste
1/2 tsp cumin powder
pinch of red chilli powder, optional

1. Pomegranate seeds are housed in the entire fruit of the pomegranate. To remove seeds easily, cut the crown end off the pomegranate, then lightly score the rind from top to bottom five or six times around the fruit.

2. Immerse the fruit in a bowl of water and soak five minutes. Hold the fruit under water (which prevents juice from spattering) and break sections apart.

3. Next, separate seeds from the rind and membrane. Seeds will sink to the bottom of the bowl; rind and membrane will float. Skim off and discard the rind and membrane. Drain seeds, then pat dry.

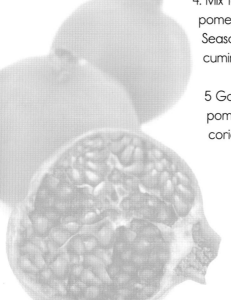

4. Mix together the yoghurt, most of the pomegranate seeds and fresh coriander. Season with salt, lots of black pepper, the cumin and red chilli powder.

5 Garnish with a handful of pomegranate seeds and a few coriander leaves.

Raitas & Chutneys

Mango Chutney

Ingredients

3-4 green mangoes (cut into chunks)
150g/3/4 cup of light muscovado sugar
1 red chilli (scored open)
150ml/2/3 cup of cider vinegar
1 inch piece of fresh root ginger (grated)
1 clove of garlic (crushed)
5 cardamom pods (bruised)
1/2 tsp coriander seeds (crushed)
1/2 tsp salt
1 bay leaf

Directions

1. Place the mango in a saucepan and pour over the cider vinegar. Cover and heat over a low/medium heat for 10-12 minutes.

2. Stir in the sugar, chilli, ginger, garlic, cardamom pods, coriander seeds, bay leaf and salt, gradually bringing the mixture to the boil, stirring frequently.

3. Reduce the heat and simmer gently for 30-35 minutes, until the mixture is thick and syrupy. Remove from the heat and set aside to cool.

4. Once cooled, transfer into a hot, glass jar and cover securely. Leave for 1 week before using.

Apple & Mango Chutney

Ingredients

250g/9oz raw mangoes (peeled and sliced)
250g/9oz cooking apples (peeled and sliced)
2 big cardamoms (crushed)
225ml/1 cup vinegar
225ml/1 cup water
1/2 tsp red chilli powder
260g/1 3/4 cups sugar
3 tsps salt
4 cloves garlic
1 tsp ginger
4 tsps raisins
8 almonds (blanched)

Directions

1. Cook the mangoes and apples in water with ginger and garlic until tender and the water is absorbed.

2. Add the vinegar, sugar, almonds, red chilli powder, cardamoms and raisins and cook on a medium heat until of a thick consistency.

Tomato Chutney

Ingredients

6 large vine-ripened tomatoes
1 large red onion (finely chopped)
2 handfuls of fresh coriander (finely chopped)
1 tbsp olive oil
1 tsp cumin seeds

Directions

1. Halve the tomatoes, remove the seeds, chop the flesh and place in a sieve over a bowl so the excess juices can drain away.

2. Put the onion and coriander into a bowl. Heat the oil and fry the cumin seeds for about 30 seconds then tip them into the bowl. Mix in the tomatoes, then allow to chill. To serve, add some salt and serve.

Tamarind * & Jaggery Chutney

Ingredients
3/4 tsp cumin seeds
2 tsps tamarind paste
3-4 tbsps jaggery (chopped)
1/2 tsp freshly ground black pepper
pinch salt
70ml/2fl oz water
6 mint leaves, shredded (optional)

Directions
1. Heat the cumin seeds in a frying pan and dry fry for 1-2 minutes, or until fragrant and golden-brown.

2. Transfer to a pestle and mortar and grind to a powder.

3. Put all of the ingredients into a small pan and mix until well combined. Bring the mixture to the boil, then reduce the heat to a simmer and simmer for 3-5 minutes, or until the mixture has thickened. Set aside to cool.

4. Serve as a dip, ideally with samosas.

* Tamarind is the seed pods from the tamarind tree. It is widely used to provide a sweet and tart flavour to savoury meat and vegetable dishes and in drinks and deserts in South Asia. India is the top producer, growing tamarind in orchard-like plantations for domestic use and export. Tamarind paste provides a distinctive authentic flavour. A key ingredient alongside other spices found in indian, thai and chinese food.

If you cannot find tamarind paste, you can substitute the following: for 1 tablespoon paste substitute 1 1/2 tablespoons amchur powder or 1 tablespoon Worcestershire sauce.

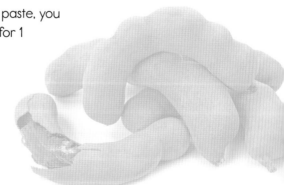

Green Tomato Chutney

Ingredients
1 tbsp root ginger
8-10 chillies
2kg/4lb green tomatoes (chopped)
500g/1lb apples (peeled, cored and chopped)
250g/8oz raisins (chopped)
625g/1 1/4lb shallots (chopped)
2 tsps salt
500g/1lb brown sugar
570ml/1 pint malt vinegar

Directions
1. Bruise the ginger and tie in a muslin bag with the chillies.

2. Place all the other ingredients in a preserving pan and suspend the muslin bag among them.

3. Bring to the boil, stirring until the sugar has dissolved, and simmer until the desired consistency is reached.

4. Remove the muslin bag. Pour into warmed sterilised jars, cover and label.

Spring Onion Raita

Ingredients
4 spring onions (chopped in iced water, which makes them crisp)
2 tbsps finely chopped coriander stalks
1/4 tsp sugar
salt and freshly ground black pepper
4 tbsps thick yoghurt

To garnish
1/2 tsp roasted ground cumin seeds

Directions
1. Soak the chopped spring onions in iced water for 30 minutes. Drain and pat dry with a cloth (or you can take them straight from the fridge).

2. Combine the remaining ingredients and stir in the spring onions.

3. Garnish with roasted ground cumin seeds and serve immediately.

Spiced Carrot Chutney

Ingredients
500g/1lb 2oz carrots
1/2 tsp/15g Red chili pepper
2 long strips/30g fresh ginger
2 cloves garlic
8 blanched almonds, halved
4 tsps/60g raisins
4 tsps salt
360g/2 cups sugar
3/4 tsp crushed cardamoms
225ml/1 cup pickling vinegar
225ml/1 cup water

Directions
1. Scrape and grate the carrots, chop the garlic and slice the ginger into long strips. Put the grated carrots, water, garlic and ginger in a deep pan and cook on a slow heat until tender and water is absorbed. Stir well.

2. Add the vinegar, sugar, salt, raisins, almonds and crushed cardamoms and cook till a little thick. Pour in a clean jar and secure tightly. Best served after at least 2 days, as this gives the flavours time to develop.

Cucumber and Curried Pea Raita

Ingredients for curry relish
150g/5oz shelled peas
1 tbsp coriander seeds
2 1/2 tbsps olive oil
1 onion, very finely chopped
2 tbsps Madras curry powder
pinch of salt
1 red chilli, finely diced

Ingredients for raita
1 tsp salt
2 cucumbers
250g/1 cup of natural yoghurt
75ml/1/3 cup water
10 tsps milk
5 spring onions, white parts only

1. Bring a small pan of salted water to a boil. Cook the peas in the water until bright green. Drain and set aside. In a dry frying pan over a medium flame, toast the coriander seeds.

2. Crush the seeds with a rolling pin or in a pestle and mortar. Set them aside. Heat the olive oil in a frying pan over medium-high heat. Add the onion, curry powder and salt. Let it cook until the onions are translucent and soft - about 10 minutes.

3. Add the chilli and cook for another minute, then add the peas and the coriander seeds and cook for two minutes to let the flavours infuse. Remove from heat and allow to cool.

4. To make the raita, peel the cucumbers and scoop out their seeds with a spoon. Cut them into medium chunks (1cm or so). Place them in a blender with the other raita ingredients. Purée until smooth.

5. To serve, put a generous spoonful of peas and onions in centre of each bowl of raita.

Lime Pickle
Ingredients
4 green limes
1 inch piece root ginger, sliced
1 tbsp white vinegar
10 cayenne chillies sliced
2 tbsps sugar
1 tbsp paprika
1 tsp garam masala
1 tsp cumin seeds

Lime Pickle/cont.
2 cloves garlic, sliced
2 tsps salt
2 tbsps oil

Directions
1. Quarter the limes. Place in a large jar with 1 tsp of salt and seal. Mix the salt up by shaking then leave in a sunny spot for 3-4 days. Move the jar round regularly.

2. Add the rest of the salt to the jar, mix, and leave for 1 month in the sun. Rotate the jar every day. Heat some oil in a pan and cook the ginger till golden. Now add the vinegar, limes and lime juice from the jar.

3. Mix well and cook for about 5 minutes. Add the spices, garlic and chillies, and cook for a further 3 minutes. Store in sterilised jars and keep in the fridge for up to 1 month.

Index

index

Spoons to millilitres

1/2 Teaspoon	2.5ml	1 Tablespoon	15ml
1 Teaspoon	5ml	2 Tablespoons	30ml
1-1/2 Teaspoons	7.5ml	3 Tablespoons	45ml
2 Teaspoons	10 ml	4 Tablespoons	60ml

Grams to Ounces

10g	0.25oz	225g	8oz
15g	0.38oz	250g	9oz
25g	1oz	275g	10oz
50g	2oz	300g	11oz
75g	3oz	350g	12oz
110g	4oz	375g	13oz
150g	5oz	400g	14oz
175g	6oz	425g	15oz
200g	7oz	450g	16oz

Metric to Cups

Flour etc	115g	1 cup
Clear Honey etc	350g	1 cup
Liquids	225ml	1 cup

Liquid measures

5fl oz	1/4 pint	150ml
7.5fl oz		215ml
10fl oz	1/2 pint	275ml
15fl oz		425ml
20fl oz	1 pint	570ml
35fl oz	1-3/4 pints	1 litre

Conversions

Temperature

Celsius	Farenheit	Gas Mark	Description
110c	225F	1/4	very cool
130c	250F	1/2	very cool
140c	275F	1	cool
150c	300F	2	cool
170c	325F	3	very moderate
180c	350F	4	moderate
190c	375F	5	moderate
200c	400F	6	moderately hot
220c	425F	7	hot
230c	450F	8	hot
240c	475F	9	very hot

Conversions